Praise for *On Silver Tides*

'Timely in its theme of protecting our rivers and streams, it also
has the timeless power and craftsmanship of a classic'
Nicolette Jones, *The Sunday Times*, Book of the Week

'A shimmering, stark, original novel, richly
characterised and unforgettably atmospheric'
Guardian

'A timely environmental message underpins this
beautifully written adventure . . . Broodingly atmospheric,
this is a richly imagined world'
Daily Mail

'A haunting, lyrical fable . . . Beautiful and thought-provoking'
Irish Times

'This book is a gift of rare imagination and luminous writing.
On Silver Tides is a classic in the making and I loved every word'
Katya Balen

'Bishop's writing transforms Britain into a magical network of
rivers, channels and lochs that will fill you with wonder'
Ann Sei Lin

'I loved this book so much. It feels to me like a
contemporary classic: thoughtful, literary, with clear
and gorgeous prose, yet urgent and relevant'
Alice Winn

'The kind of storytelling that stops your breath and weaves knots
around your heart. Exquisite, and hard to leave behind'
Nicola Penfold

UNDER GOLDEN SEAS

UNDER GOLDEN SEAS

SYLVIA BISHOP

ANDERSEN PRESS

First published in Great Britain in 2025 by
Andersen Press Limited
6 Coptic Street, London, WC1A 1NH, UK
Vijverlaan 48, 3062 HL Rotterdam, Nederland
www.andersenpress.co.uk

2 4 6 8 10 9 7 5 3 1

All rights reserved. No part of this publication may be reproduced,
stored in a retrieval system or transmitted in any form, or by
any means, electronic, mechanical, photocopying, recording
or otherwise, without the written permission of the publisher.

The right of Sylvia Bishop to be identified as the author of
this work has been asserted by her in accordance with the Copyright,
Designs and Patents Act, 1988.

Copyright © Sylvia Bishop, 2025
Map © Rebecca Freeman, 2025

British Library Cataloguing in Publication Data available.

ISBN 978 1 83913 498 2

Printed and bound in Great Britain by Clays Ltd, Elcograf S.p.A.

*For the elves at no. 4
who are So Good*

1

Asleep, Dylan had been entirely human. Now rain had woken him, and inside his body, something else was stirring.

He pulled his blankets over his head, willing himself to sink back into the dream he had been having. He had forgotten it already, but he knew it had been warm and kind. Underneath him, the mattress was soft; outside his bed, the air was cold and unwelcoming.

But the rain on the roof was getting harder, and the stirring grew more urgent. It made his bones ache, and his blood was growing thicker now, making his pulse feel swollen and heavy. His thoughts were unsteady, as though they were already tumbling through the churn of waves.

He gave in, and sat up.

The house was quiet. His family would be sleeping; he was the only one who woke like this when it rained. They were in better control of their sea-selves. He should be too. He could just lie back down, and ignore it.

His small human insides seemed to lurch and spin. With no room for thought, he put out a hand for the dressing gown he kept near the bed, and slipped it on. Then he stood, ducked out of his bedroom, and padded barefoot down the stairs.

On the floor below he passed his family's bedrooms, and hesitated.

He wanted someone to come with him. He avoided going to sea alone whenever he could. Once, when he was nine, he had attacked a man in the water; for three awful days, it had been uncertain whether the man would live. Now, when Dylan's sea-self gripped him like this in the night, he felt a surge of panic – as though the man was still dying.

But since then, everyone said, his control had improved. He had been so young, they said. It was seven years ago, and it wasn't a problem anymore. He could go to sea alone without being a danger. If he woke anyone now, that's what they would say.

And mostly, his control did seem to have improved. He had never hurt anyone else. And he hardly ever woke in the night like this nowadays, compelled by rain. Hardly ever.

He grew more lucid as he stood in the cold hallway, shivering. His family, he remembered, were leaving the house early tomorrow – there was business at sea for his parents, and his twin sisters would go too, now that they were of age. He *definitely* shouldn't wake them up in the middle of the night, then. Maybe he could resist this urge. He could prove that he was in control, like they all said, and just go back to bed.

As though it heard him, the rain intensified. Wind flung it hard against the window at the end of the landing. Drops blurred into one great sheet of water; thoughts blurred in Dylan, and he stumbled forwards.

He was not a child: he could go alone. He left his family sleeping, and half fell down the stairs.

In the front room, there was a snore, which made him start. He had forgotten that his uncle was visiting, and sleeping in a hammock slung from the beams. More softly, he crossed to the door, opened it, slipped out, and gently closed it again. Then he set off, down through the pine trees, to the shore of Loch Ness.

Sometimes, nights on the loch were still and wide and wonderful. Tonight, the wind and rain made it a wild, inhospitable place. The water tore at itself in uneasy waves, and the rain drove sideways against Dylan as he hurried to the shore. Under its influence, the ache in his bones became unbearably heavy, and his heart thumped as though it was trying to burst him open. He stumbled a little as he neared the water's edge. Hurriedly, he took off dressing gown and pyjamas, stowing them in the box his family kept there.

Then he made himself slow down. If he could choose the moment when he went into the water, that proved he was in control. And if he was in control, he would not hurt anybody. So at the edge of the loch, he focused all his will power, and stood still.

He was excited now. The warmth of bed was forgotten. He could almost sense the salt-tang of the sea, the swell of the waves . . .

He instructed himself to notice human feelings. Smooth cold shingle under his feet. The bite of the wind on his thin skin. He held back: one second. Two seconds. Three.

Then he let these small thoughts fall away, and stepped into the loch.

There was a flare of light, and the human boy was gone. The waves were pushed aside by a vast v-shaped wake on the water, as something enormous moved beneath the surface. Then it sank deeper and disappeared, crossing the bottom of the loch towards the river and the sea, leaving only the waves, and the rain.

The first time the v-shaped trail re-appeared, it was at the far side of the loch. The wind had dropped, and a thin dawn was beginning; the water was still and silver. A gaggle of geese were sleeping nearby, and two children were swimming.

When one of the children screamed, it woke the geese, who threw up a confusion of honking and flapping. Blood spread rapidly across the water, black in the half-light.

The second child hauled their friend to the shore, yelling for help, sobbing about monsters in the loch. Behind them, the ripples disappeared.

The second time the trail appeared, it was at the shore below the cottage once again, and the morning light was strong and golden overhead. A moment later, Dylan was back on land.

It was like waking, the murky half-memories of the water slipping away like dreams, his human thoughts arriving piece by piece. There, those were his small toes on the round grey stones. There, that was land-light, steady and still in the way that sea-light never was. He crouched on the shingle for a minute, feeling warm sun on soft skin, and breathing deeply.

He could remember getting up in the night and coming down to the shore, but even that had the quality of a fever dream. After that, his memories quickly faded. This was why he didn't like to go alone: there was no one who could tell him, with certainty, that he had done no harm.

But there was no use regretting his weakness now. He stood, and stretched. He searched one last time, fruitlessly, for any memories of the night. He reminded himself that he had hurt nobody for seven full, peaceful years.

He wanted a cup of tea, and company. He set off through the trees for home.

THE SEA WEARD

FROM *THE SEA AND ITS CITIZENS*, DRAFT MANUSCRIPT

The Sea is a world utterly unlike our own. It is vast and alien and cruel.

The River Lore says: 'Let the landmen guard the water in the ground; let the silvermen guard the water in the Rivers; let all men fear the Sea.' Thankfully, the Sea Lore is somewhat more helpful, and gives advice for the Sea Weard – the guardians of our shores. Thanks to the Weard, many former terrors are only remembered as stories today: the blue-men and the bucca, the ceirean and the murigen, the nuckelavee and the tangie and the seonaidh.

The Lore says that the office of Sea Weard must be held by two wyrms. Wyrms are shapeshifters, living primarily in human form, and they have been given many names over the centuries: water-dragons, loch monsters, knuckers, uilebheists and sea-serpents, to name some of the least offensive. In their water-form they are enormous, which has led at times to fear and persecution – both from silvermen, who understand what they are, and from landmen, who can only guess.

The strength of wyrms is necessary to meet the threats at sea. Their minds are fully human, and so they are capable of great self-control when at sea: there is no reason to believe they are a danger to humans.

2

It was a bright October morning now. Dylan's body felt fresh and new, but his unease was a solid thing, sitting lumpishly at the top of his lungs. He had not felt a sea urge like that in a long time. It meant that his control was slipping.

Everybody would say that it wasn't important. But Mam's eyes would be soft with worry, and Dad would go all hearty and jolly, and Tor would want to fuss over him as if she thought that she alone had noticed he was upset. Meriel might genuinely shrug it off. Sometimes, Meriel's permanent residence inside her own world was helpful.

Halfway up the bank he remembered that the family would be getting ready to leave. He stopped stupidly in his tracks. Then he changed direction slightly, making for the back door. Everyone would already be stressed. It was better if he could avoid worrying them all – if he could pretend he'd just woken up, having slumbered peacefully through the rain like the rest of them.

He looped through the pines a little distance from the house, only coming closer when he could make a beeline for the back door without passing a window. The trees cast long morning shadows here, and he didn't spot the kelpie until it stepped out right in front of him.

'Dylan Pade,' it said.

This was, Dylan thought, the last thing he needed.

Kelpies were shapeshifters too: sometimes human, sometimes horse, sometimes wind, and almost always annoying. They were more wind, in reality, than anything else, and the human form was only skin-deep. They had a reputation as fortune tellers, but Dylan had never heard one say anything useful. This one looked like a man – a skinny naked man, with matted hair and sombre eyes.

'Dylan Pade,' it said solemnly.

'Yep, that's me,' he said. 'Anything else?'

'Dylan Pade,' repeated the kelpie.

'Right,' said Dylan. 'Well, thanks for that.' And he carried on up the bank towards the house, trying to ignore the kelpie staring morosely at his back. Now he had two things not to tell the family about. His mam *hated* kelpies.

At the house he glanced back. It had taken a few steps forward, and was watching him go. He made a rude gesture to relieve his feelings, but it just blinked back at him.

Softly, he opened the back door. Their house was a small, red brick cottage – the gingerbread cottage, they called it. It smelled of the sharp pine tar they used to protect the wood from damp, mingled once a week with the smell of laundry soap. The back door led straight into a crowded utility room, where the family kept the sea creatures they were studying, and this opened out on to a short hallway; from there, Dylan could arrive in the kitchen or front room as though he had just come down the stairs. He wouldn't have to outright lie. He just wouldn't have to announce his arrival.

He shut the back door, very gently. To his right, a sunfish stared at him with its *oh-no* expression. Dylan liked sunfish. He did his best impression of an *oh-no* face right back.

'Good morning,' said his uncle.

Dylan started, and spun around.

Uncle Firth straightened up from his squat, where he had been regarding the jellyfish tank with interest, and looked at Dylan. Uncle and nephew were remarkably alike, on the surface: they both had the same broad face and thick dark hair, although Uncle Firth's stuck up at more inconvenient angles. But looks were deceiving. Uncle Firth was an ordinary silverman – amphibious but fully human, living on his boat on the freshwater rivers with the rest of his kind, and following the River Lore. Salt water would kill him. He didn't have a sea-self, or get desperate urges in the rain, or receive bothersome morning calls from kelpies.

He did, however, share one important thing with Dylan. He had nearly caused his sister Isla's death, when they were young – a buried family story that they rarely spoke of now. That was before Mam had been infected, like Dad, with the eel-sickness that had made them both wyrms; and it was long before their monstrous children had been born. The time Dylan had attacked a man, and nothing would console him, Mam had taken him to see Uncle Firth.

'I detect stealth . . . ?' his uncle murmured now, eyebrows raised.

'I've been to sea,' whispered Dylan. 'I don't want to worry everyone.'

'You're not a burden, Dylan.' His uncle's response was reflexive, immediate.

'I know – I just – I'd rather not talk to everyone about it. Not now. Maybe when they're back.'

Uncle Firth gave this a second's consideration, then shrugged. 'You won't worry anyone,' he said. 'But they don't need to know, either. Your decision.'

'Thanks,' said Dylan. He jerked his head towards the rest of the house. 'How's it all going?'

'Well, I think the plan was to leave by nine, but Tor's dropped a pan on her foot and Meriel isn't awake yet.'

'Sounds about right.'

'I recommend hiding from it all with the jellyfish. They're very soothing.'

'I might take you up on that,' said Dylan, 'once I've had some tea.' With a grateful smile, he opened the door to check that the coast was clear, and slipped into the hall. He gave his dressing gown a few quick strokes, in case of any pine needles or mud. Then he sidled innocently into the kitchen, where Tor sat on the counter. She had one foot in the sink, and was patting it ineffectually with a dead haddock.

'Morning,' she said cheerfully. 'There's a kelpie outside!'

Dylan remembered in time not to know this, and not to know about dropping the pan. He made an interested sort of 'Mm?' about the kelpie, which was believable – only Tor would act like this was exciting – and nodded at her foot. 'Why the fish?' he asked. This was, in fact, a genuine question.

'The ice in the box is all gone, this was the coldest thing I could find,' said Tor. She was immediately disconsolate, as though she had forgotten her swelling foot and only this moment remembered it. Tor and Meriel's faces were identical, but Meriel's never went through the rapid emotional turbulence of Tor's. 'I dropped my porridge pan on it. I'm meant to be helping with the nets and now I'm making us late and Mam's all tense.'

Dylan carefully filled the copper kettle around the obstacle of Tor's knee, and said, 'How many times has Dad said "time and tide"?' Whenever the family were late, Dylan's dad liked to quote a landman saying about time and tide waiting for no man. The later they got, the more heartily he said it.

'Oh, a million,' said Tor. 'Are you making tea? Can I have some?'

'Yep.' Dylan had anticipated this, and had already filled the kettle generously. He put it on the stove. Through the window, from a distance, he saw that the kelpie was staring at them. Or, more accurately, at him. It adjusted itself slightly to get a better view.

The lump of unease began to thicken again, just below his throat now. Traditionally, a kelpie following you around was not a good omen. Dylan breathed, trying to squash down the panic. He had just gone to sea, that was all. That had only ever gone wrong once, and it had been years ago.

Still.

He almost told Tor. She was good at giving comfort, if you were in the mood for it. When he had been little, if Mam and Dad were away, it was Tor he ran to. But just as he was opening his mouth, Mam came in.

'Morning, smallest monster,' she said to Dylan – then to Tor, 'How's it looking?'

Tor took the fish away and considered this. 'Red. Biggish.'

'Oof,' said Mam, inspecting the damage. 'You should be elevating it – I don't think that haddock is doing anything, love. Dylan, could you help with the nets? Actually – can you try and rouse Meriel first?'

Dad followed in behind her. 'Full fathom five my daughter lies,' he said, misquoting landman poetry. 'A medal if you can wake her. Ah, are you making tea?'

Dylan had been reaching for a couple of the larger mugs, but he nodded, and took down three medium-sized ones instead.

'Aah-*ow*,' said Tor behind him. She had eased herself down from the counter, then immediately stumbled sideways.

'Don't put weight on it yet!' Mam commanded. 'Tea for me too, please. Can someone *please* wake Meriel?'

Dylan took down a fourth, slightly smaller mug. 'I'll get her,' he said. 'Kettle's almost boiled. Can someone make me one?' And he left everyone to their haddocks and kettles and poetry, and went back upstairs. It was good to get away from the crush, and the kelpie's stare. Their house was always cold, but he had been suddenly too hot.

Upstairs, in his sisters' room, it was quiet. He could hear the distant hush and sigh of the loch. Meriel looked so peaceful that Dylan didn't like to wake her; tucked up under the covers, with her long red plaits snaking over her pillow, she looked very young. He felt a sudden wave of the back-to-front homesickness that came when everyone went away at once.

He squatted beside the bed. 'Merri,' he said gently, putting a hand on the blanket bundle. 'Merri, wake up. You have to get ready to go.'

'Mmminutemore,' murmured Meriel.

Dad was right – she was particularly deeply asleep today. Two things could get through to Meriel, as a general rule: the sea, and Tor. 'You're going to the Sargasso Sea today,' Dylan tried.

'Mmm,' said Meriel.

'You'll swim through the Azores,' Dylan added. 'And maybe you'll solve the eel question.'

Meriel snuffled something incoherent.

He would have to play his trump card, then. 'Tor's hurt her foot,' he said.

Meriel's eyes snapped open at once, bleary but awake. 'She'lright?' she mumbled.

Dylan shrugged. 'Looks painful.'

Meriel's body was upright before her brain had really caught up; she blinked in confusion, as though not sure how she'd got there. 'What'd she do?' she asked.

But Dylan wasn't going to lose his advantage that easily. He stood and turned for the door, saying, 'Come and see.'

At the stairs he paused: for a moment he almost wondered if it had failed. Then he heard Meriel's footsteps shuffling behind him. He smiled. They both went downstairs to the kitchen.

Tor was alone again, gazing out at the kelpie with interest, clutching her tea with both hands. A spare mug sat on the counter, steam spiralling upwards.

'Ooh good,' said Meriel, picking it up. '*Tea*. Tor, are you OK?'

Dylan reminded himself that he would miss everyone painfully very soon, took a breath, and refilled the kettle.

Five minutes later there was peace. Tor had declared herself fit as a fiddle, and had been helped to the front room by Meriel, determined to get back to work on the nets; Uncle Firth had cautiously emerged, and installed himself in an armchair with a book; Dylan had tea at last, and joined the rest of the family at the table to knot the silver threads.

Silver weakens most salt-water creatures. The job of the Weard is to protect the British Isles from the threats at sea – the coastal predators that terrorise landmen; the storm-born hunters that come in by sea to lurk in caves and springs; the troublesome spirits that can invade our rivers; and the more distant and ancient creatures that could distort whole seas and threaten all life. Some things in the sea are difficult or impossible to destroy, and need to be bound instead – caught in a trap that weakens them for a time, until the next binding. For the stronger creatures, you need the purity of sea-silver, which is found at seabed springs. It works best freshly forged, so the Pades' threads were always made at the last moment, then quickly knotted into nets.

As they worked, Uncle Firth scribbled notes from the book he was reading. He was writing a book on the sea for silvermen. It was already several volumes long. The fact that other silvermen generally viewed the project with disinterest, disapproval, or occasionally disgust did not deter him: Uncle Firth could be stubborn sometimes. Mam glanced at the clock now and then as they worked, but she was never really stressed once work was underway. Dylan often marvelled that the practical, efficient pairing of Mam and Dad could have produced the chaos of Tor – or Meriel, who trailed so far behind the pace of the world that Dad still called her Little Echo, even now. Dylan was the youngest child, but he often felt like the oldest. On land, at any rate.

In the middle of a comfortable silence, Uncle Firth paused his scribbling, and looked up from his book. 'That's odd,' he said. 'Your almanac says this nál wasn't due for a binding until next year . . . ?'

Mam snipped a thread, and said, 'It got loose early. It happens sometimes. We had word from our kind in the Americas that a landman ship went missing.' Binding the nál, a large and ancient spirit-eater, was a job for the wyrms of all the Seas, not just the British Weard.

'Náls eat landmen?' said Uncle Firth, appalled.

'Omnivorous spirit-eater,' said Dad. 'It's not fussy.'

'They call that bit of the Atlantic the Bermuda Triangle,' said Tor, who was especially fond of landmen.

'It's the Sargasso Sea,' said Meriel – especially fond, as always, of the Sea. She paused mid-knot, hands frozen as though conjuring. 'It's a weird place. The Lore says all the eels in our rivers are born there and they go back there to die but we haven't worked out where exactly, or why. It's one of my projects . . .'

Uncle Firth raised his eyebrows, impressed. 'Long way for an eel to go.'

'Long way for a wyrm to go,' said Mam. She looked at the clock once more, and at the pile of finished netting. 'I'd like to have made more, but I think we should go when we've finished this net. I really want to avoid night travel.'

Dad nodded. 'We're out of sea-silver anyway,' he said. 'This is the last of it.'

'Really?'

'Remember we used some on the rogue mither?'

'Ah,' said Mam, nodding. 'Well, that settles that then. Girls, will you be ready when this is done?'

Tor immediately remembered ten things she wanted to do, and went hobbling off; two minutes later it occurred to Meriel that she hadn't fed any of her most beloved creatures in the utility room yet, and she too drifted away. But this was just the last quiet rippling of chaos. By the time the nets were stowed on the bandoleers, the twins were back in the front room, ready to leave.

'Right,' said Mam. 'Toast.' And she took the cordial down from the shelf, and unstoppered it, while Dad lined up the glasses.

'Join us, Firth?' said Dad. 'It's a passing-toast, a bit like River ones. A little bit of tradition from the Lore.'

The Sea Lore was a book from the Weards of the past, with advice on the Sea. More than half of it had rotted away over the centuries, and what was left was only partially reliable. But the instructions for this ritual had remained intact.

Mam poured out the glasses, and Tor started handing them round. Then they all stood in the middle of their front room in a circle, and looked at each other. Mam smiled. The clock ticked loudly, but for a moment, the little circle of Pades felt still: purposeful and unhurried.

'You're probably east, Doug,' said Mam, assessing. 'Start us off.'

So Dad turned to Mam, and with great mock-solemnity, raised his glass. 'O Kelda Pade, my beloved monster, Weard of the Sea, and of both my hearts . . .'

Mam feigned exasperation. 'Get on with it, or I'll have to drink my own.'

'You wound me.'

'You'll live.'

Dad sighed theatrically, then held out the glass towards her. They both held on to it, hands meeting, while Dad recited: 'Kelda Pade. May the Sea keep your spirit in blood.'

'May the Sea keep your spirit in bone,' replied Mam. Her face had softened in the way it sometimes did, without warning – it made her look suddenly younger, and vulnerable, and so full of love that it almost hurt to look at.

'May the Sea keep your spirit in breath,' said Dad.

Then Mam let go of the glass, and Dad held it to her lips for her to drink. When it was all gone, she picked up her own full glass and turned to Tor – her face still soft – and began again. 'Torlan Pade. May the Sea keep your spirit in blood . . .'

They went round the whole circle like this. Tor passed to

Meriel, who passed to Dylan, who turned to Uncle Firth, and hesitated. Uncle Firth was a silverman, and belonged to the River. Would he want a strange Sea blessing?

'Go on,' said Uncle Firth, seeing the hesitation. 'I don't have as much spirit as you lot. I need any protection I can get.'

Dylan smiled. 'Then, Firth Pade,' he said, 'may the Sea keep your spirit in blood.'

Uncle Firth nodded, smiling back at his monstrous nephew. 'May the Sea keep your spirit in bone.'

'May the Sea keep your spirit in breath.'

Dylan raised the glass and Uncle Firth downed his drink, spluttered, and coughed for a good twenty seconds. Dylan whacked him on the back a few times, but it was not at all clear whether this helped. When he finally wheezed to a halt, there were tears in his eyes. 'River and moon, Kelda,' he said, 'what's *in* that?'

'I added a little sea ginger,' said Mam. And when Uncle Firth looked woundedly at her, she said, 'Only a little. Maybe it's an acquired taste.'

'Yes,' he said, 'I think it is.'

'Consider yourself lucky,' said Dad. 'The Lore has instructions for adding silver to the cordial. We've decided against ritual stomach aches, on balance.'

'A blessing,' Uncle Firth croaked. 'I'm going to get some water . . .'

He broke the circle to go to the kitchen, and instantly the spell-like stillness broke too. There was an efficient urgency now to the family's movements as they took up the bandoleers, slung them across their chests and checked the fastenings.

The bandoleers were made from several loops of silver chain, designed to unspool into a single loop when their bodies changed, and were used to carry their tools and supplies. His sisters looked much older, suddenly, going through the same practised motions as Mam and Dad: the Weard, and the Weard-in-waiting.

Dylan wanted to join them. His parents insisted he waited until he was of age, as though it was the work of the Weard that should frighten him. But he wasn't remotely frightened of the sea. He was only frightened of being left here, alone. As he watched them, the unease he had felt at the loch came back, sudden and overwhelming. He didn't want to be alone with his sea-self, it was too strong. What if he needed to go to sea again, with no one here to keep him under control? He would ask Uncle Firth to lock the doors, hide the key, hold him down . . .

'Bye, love,' said Mam, hugging him. And, as though she could read his thoughts, she added, 'We'll be back before you know it.'

Dylan squeezed her back, the cold bandoleer between them; he squeezed all his family; Uncle Firth came back, and there were more goodbyes, and an extra hug for Dylan from Tor as she whispered, 'We'll miss you, we'll be back so soon'. And then all goodbyes were done, and the family turned like a shoal towards the front door.

But before they could leave, the window imploded.

Glass shards flew inwards, but didn't fall as they should; they spiralled into the room, born on a sudden wild wind. The wind raced about the room, howling round the beams, tipping chairs and spilling cordial, sending books and sea-maps flying.

'What the—' said Dad, ducking.

Mam's fists were balled up in hatred. 'River and *moon*,' she said. 'That *salting* kelpie!'

SHAPESHIFTERS AND SPIRIT
FROM *THE SEA AND ITS CITIZENS*, DRAFT MANUSCRIPT

All living things create spirit: it is found in blood, bone and breath. Loose spirit may also be found where the world moves quickly – in winds and currents and waves. Sometimes spirit can be passed from one creature to another, through bites or wounds; it can also be eaten, by specialised predators.

Those we call 'shapeshifters' have more than one kind of spirit, forcing their bodies to take more than one form. Sometimes – but not always – these forms are tied to particular places (for example, to the water and the land), or to phases of the moon, or to seasons.

Shapeshifters have nothing else particular in common with each other, and while our closest cousins – the wyrms – are truly people, others are better understood as animals (for example, selkies – notwithstanding their convincing human forms) or elements (for example, kelpies – which are more obviously inhuman). It is outdated, and somewhat offensive, to consider shapeshifters a single 'type'. Indeed, in their daily lives, they are frequently at odds with each other.

3

For a minute they all grabbed at random objects uselessly, as the kelpie wreaked havoc across the front room. Meriel lunged head-first into the wind to protect books; Mam lunged to protect Meriel, and they were both promptly gusted backwards on to the floor.

'D'you think it wants to tell us something?' said Tor. But no one else had any interest in what the kelpie might or might not want; they were a little busy trying not to get concussed by anything falling from the shelves. For a brief moment there was a horse in the room, rearing and rolling its eyes, then a howling man, and then the wild wind returned.

'Can't you use the nets on it?' yelled Uncle Firth, diving out of the way of a toppling coat stand.

'The shapeshifters of the River are outside our domain,' said Tor, quoting the Lore, and looking a little scandalised at the suggestion.

'It's bad form, Firth,' shouted Dad. 'You've got to respect—'

'The utility room!' yelped Dylan, running to the hall – but the wind had gusted on ahead of him, and he was too late.

There was an almighty shattering of glass and gushing of water, as the wind spirit flung itself around the tanks and jars and vials. Everyone rushed out into the hall, crying out for their own most-beloved experiment – except Uncle Firth, who was still at the table, trying to mop up the invaluable map. The rest of them crowded behind Dylan, and stared helplessly.

It was the sort of mess that paralyses the mind. Puddles oozed – water, formaldehyde, squid ink, blood. Gasping sea-creatures lay everywhere. The whole scene was sprinkled with shattered glass and spilled silver, glittering where squares of light fell through the two skylights. And in amongst it all, a mass of tiny sea leeches coiled and writhed.

Meriel began frantically scooping up the most beloved of her fish, shaking off the leeches that immediately came questing for her hands. Everybody else's brains seemed to have broken. Even the kelpie-wind fell still a moment, as though it had surprised itself.

'Oh, this will be hours of work,' Mam was saying. 'We won't even be leaving till dusk now . . .'

'Me and Uncle Firth can fix it,' said Dylan, nodding at his uncle, who had come to join them.

Dad shook his head. 'I'm not leaving you two alone with this mess. Kelda –' he put a hand on Mam's shoulder – 'you three get going. I'll help Dyl and follow on behind.'

Mam looked at him, and Dylan could almost see the mental risk-maths taking place in her eyes.

'I'll be fine,' said Dad. 'You know I will. And you'll be all the protection the girls need, as long as the three of you can travel in the light.' Wyrms kept growing well into adulthood;

Meriel and Tor were big, but Mam and Dad were enormous. 'We can't leave Dylan alone with all of this.'

Uncle Firth looked slightly offended at this, but then stepped on a sea-slug and leaped back in horror with a squeal – which made it difficult to protest.

'Right,' said Mam. 'Yes. Should we stay and help with the start . . . ?'

'Go now. If it's just the three of you, you don't want any night travel.'

'All right. Yes. Oh, river.'

'Go, go, go. In the most loving possible way, get out, sling off across a sea, leave us alone. Meriel, Tor, do you have everything?'

Mam hugged Dylan. 'I'm sorry to rush off, Dyl. We'll see you so soon.'

'It's fine.' Dylan squeezed back, but then pushed her gently away. 'Go, I've got to find us gloves. Some of those things are dying.'

'Right. Yes. Of course. Girls – are you ready? Douglas, you'll come straight to the coastal shelf when you're done?'

'I'll be there tonight. We'll be done in a few hours here. Go.'

Dylan went to the kitchen cupboards to hunt for boots and gloves, so he missed everybody leaving. It felt peculiar. Normally he would stand on the shore and watch their trails across the water until they disappeared. Instead he just heard them swearing as they battled against the kelpie, which had apparently begun gusting against them in the living room; then the bang of the front door, and they were gone.

He always hated it. The cottage felt hollowed out. In the stillness, he was fairly sure that the kelpie had gusted out too.

There was no time for his back-to-front homesickness. He went back to the utility room, and gave his dad and uncle pairs of silver-thread gloves and wellingtons. They all put them on.

'Right then,' said Dad. 'Let's get to work.'

For a few seconds, they all just stared. It was impossible to know what to do first.

Then Dad said, 'Well, I suppose we'd just better start *somewhere*,' and began scooping up whatever was nearest. So Dylan did the same – and Uncle Firth too, although he was new to the creatures of the sea, and picked everything up very gingerly with a sort of fascinated horror. The gloves protected him from the sting of salt-water, but even so, he worked with care.

The living creatures they put in the few remaining tanks, and just had to hope for now that they weren't going to eat each other. Dylan began with the deep-sea fish, because they were giving him the creeps: they were boneless, and out of the water's pressure they had become horrifying misshapen blobs with drooping, agonised faces. He scooped and plopped hastily until they were all in water, then gathered up the jellyfish. It was hard to tell whether they were alive or not – they just hung about jellyishly in the tank, giving nothing away.

He very nearly stepped on Meriel's two young eels – they hadn't developed any colour yet, and still looked like pieces of water that had turned solid and started wriggling. He put them in the tank. He swept up splattered eggs, and cleared up a smashed vial of wreck-water, which made his fingers feel numb and swollen. They all stooped and plucked and scooped and swept, and in the end it took less time than Dad had predicted.

Then they were just left with the puddles, and the sea-leeches. It felt, impossibly, as though the leeches had multiplied.

'What *are* those?' said Uncle Firth, as one tried vainly to attach itself to his boot. It was smaller than a finger, ringed in shades of brown, with flared suckers at both ends.

'Common kind of spirit-eater,' said Dad. 'Just a blood-sucker – pretty harmless. Still, keep the silver gloves on. Dyl, can you find a spare jar? Maybe there's one in the kitchen?'

So Dylan went to the kitchen, and after some hunting, emptied a jar of pickled herring eggs that had gone uneaten for years. Then they scooped salt water into it from a tank, and set about the long task of rescuing the writhing leeches.

This part took as long as the rest put together. One managed to wriggle under Dylan's glove and bite, making him swear loudly; it took three minutes to prise it off with silver tweezers, and another three minutes for Uncle Firth to stop gazing at it in wonder, as it rapidly doubled in size from its spirit-feed. But at last every tiny leech had been found and plopped in the jar, and Dylan put them back on the spirit-eater shelf, next to the bone worms and a dead hag specimen. Then they all stood a minute, hands on hips, in the awkward arrested state of people who have finished a long task and forgotten how to do anything else.

'Mop?' suggested Uncle Firth.

'Ah, yes,' said Dad. 'Kitchen. Thank you, Firth.'

'I'll put the kettle on,' said Dylan.

'*Yes*,' agreed Dad and Uncle Firth at once.

So Dylan and Uncle Firth went to the kitchen, leaving Dad blinking in the utility room. Dylan knew that absent look. Dad was already far away; he was thinking of the others, and his path across the Atlantic plains, and the diminishing daylight hours.

At the kitchen sink, Dylan filled the kettle, then made way for Uncle Firth to fill the mop bucket. Through the window, from a little distance, a horse watched them. It seemed to be sulking.

'Do you think it *was* trying to say something?' said Dylan.

Dylan knew Uncle Firth hated kelpies at least as much as Mam – there had been an incident when they were young, which no one would talk about now. But even so, he was surprised at the disgust on Uncle Firth's face. It transformed him, suddenly, into someone else entirely.

His scholarly, soft-spoken uncle glowered at the kelpie, and said, 'Who salting cares?'

They had not been sitting at the table long when the landman arrived.

The Weard kept themselves apart from landmen, because of their habit of hunting sea monsters. Uncle Firth had once written a book explaining silvermen to a few trusted landmen, but even then, at Mam's insistence he had been vague about wyrms.

Normally they knocked on the door, so you had some warning. This time, there was suddenly a voice saying, 'Afternoon! What happened here, then?' without any preamble at all. They all jumped, and turned to stare. Then Dylan realised that they could hear him because the window was smashed – which must be what he was asking about. He racked his brains for a landman-appropriate excuse.

'I was throwing a ball,' he suggested. He'd heard that one in the village, once.

'Ah,' said the landman sagely – and he looked at Dad, and added, 'Boys will be boys.' Which didn't seem to mean anything at all, as far as Dylan could tell. But they all nodded wisely, because it felt like the right thing to do.

'Morning, Reg,' said Dad. He was better than the others at remembering some of the names from the nearest village – which was still miles away from the cottage. They could often go days at a time without seeing another soul. 'What brings you all the way out here?'

'Well, Douglas, I'm afraid it's not good news,' said Reg importantly. 'I've come to warn you – and ask for help. I'm driving all round the loch, warning and asking all of you folks.'

'Oh, aye?' said Dad mildly. 'What's the warning?'

Reg leaned through the window a little, and said, 'The monster's been seen again.'

Everybody tried to look the right amount of quite-interested.

'And I'm afraid it gets worse,' said Reg, shaking his head. 'Bad news, very bad.'

Dylan's stomach dropped. He knew what was coming next.

'There's been another attack.'

4

The strangest thing for Dylan was that the conversation continued to rattle on amiably with him right there, unseen and unaccused. It made him feel like a ghost.

'Oh,' said Dad softly, 'that's dreadful news.' And this, at least, required no acting. 'Who . . . ?'

'Mac Purley's little girl.'

'Is she all right?' Dylan was surprised to discover that *he* seemed to be the one asking this question. He heard his voice as though it belonged to someone else.

'We'll have to wait and see,' said Reg grimly. 'Doctor's with her now. The injuries are manageable, but she near-drowned, and he says she's not out of the woods yet – says he's worried about her lungs still. She was swimming in the loch with her brother – he saw the beast. Sensible boy too, not the kind for tall tales.'

There was a silence, slightly too long, before Dad found the wits to say, 'Terrible.'

'So what's the plan?' said Uncle Firth – then added, with a small wave, 'Hello, I'm Firth Pade – Kelda's brother.'

Reg nodded a greeting. If he noticed that this meant the

family had taken Mam's surname – a silverman tradition, not a landman one – he was too preoccupied to comment. 'We're asking everyone with a boat to bring it to the loch,' he said, 'and every able-bodied man to lend a hand, and bring weapons and nets. We'll trawl the canal in both directions. First boats are already out – we've been working all morning.'

Dad and Dylan exchanged half a panicked glance before they could stop themselves. Mam and Meriel and Tor would have travelled along the canal. Was that what the kelpie had been trying to say?

'Ah, Reg,' said Dad, shaking his head, 'I'm off to London today. And my brother-in-law here won't set foot in a boat – can't swim.' Uncle Firth nodded solemnly at this outrageous lie, and they all smiled at Reg, as though they couldn't sense his palpable annoyance. There would be gossip, of course, about the anti-social recluses in the red cottage. But they were used to that.

'What about you, lad?' Reg asked Dylan.

'My heart . . .' said Dylan, reflexively. All the Pade children were understood to have tragically weak hearts, thanks to a usefully vague condition. They had all been schooled at home to protect their health. They weren't seen at parties, and they could certainly never accept invitations to go swimming in the loch.

'Oh, aye,' said Reg. He looked back to Dad. 'You'll none of yous be helping, then?'

'I'll be glad to, when I'm back,' said Dad. 'Although God willing you'll already have found it.' Dad had gone monster-hunting before – whenever one of the family was glimpsed, it provoked a flurry of activity. Dylan got the impression Dad quite enjoyed it. Landmen had no idea what they were looking for, and sat in their tiny boats polishing weapons and airing mad theories. Dad always told the stories with great glee. But on those occasions, the family had all stayed safely out of the water.

'I hope so, Douglas, I hope so,' said Reg. 'We can't have that beast in our waters a moment longer.'

'I'll pray I'm not needed, then,' said Dad. 'But I promise, you'll have my help the moment I'm back.'

Reg nodded, not entirely appeased.

'Well,' said Dad. 'Thanks for bringing the news. I'm afraid I'd best be getting ready . . .'

'Right you are,' said Reg. 'I'll be on my way. Pleasure to meet you' – this last he said to Firth. Then with one more disgruntled nod at them all, he went stomping off to warn-and-ask elsewhere.

The family waited, a frozen tableau, until the sound of footsteps had faded. Even then, when they spoke, it was in hushed voices.

'Was it . . . ?' said Dad softly, looking at Dylan.

'Must have been me,' said Dylan. 'It was raining, and I went out.'

For once, Dad could not find anything jolly to say. He seemed poised in readiness to speak, but nothing came. Instead, Uncle Firth said anxiously, 'This hunt, if it started this morning . . . Kelda and the girls . . . ?'

'They ought to have been swimming deep, well out of reach,' said Dad. 'It would be very unlucky . . . But we can check the blood . . .'

Dylan nodded, and left for the utility room. He opened a cupboard, and took out the tin with the vials of each family member's blood; then he took down the jar of leeches, and a soiled silver glove. His hands, he noticed, were shaking. The glass vials rattled gently in the tin as he took them back to the front room.

'If the others are still alive, their blood will still have spirit, and the leeches will smell it,' Dad was explaining to Firth. 'If they ignore the blood, then . . .'

He didn't complete the thought. It was too awful to complete. Dylan took out three of the vials – Mam, Meriel, Tor – stood them upright on the table, and uncorked them. Then he gloved his hand, unscrewed the jar, and put down a handful of leeches. The one that had bitten him had now tripled in size and was pulsing happily; he put that one back in the jar.

The others writhed for a few moments in blind confusion.

Then they turned for the vials.

Two inched straight away up to Meriel's. One more straggler began for Meriel's as well, but finding it occupied, smelled its way over to Mam's.

Dylan corked up those vials, plucked off the leeches, and returned them to the table. He put the vials in the tin, and moved it away. His own blood, he noticed, was still fizzing gently: an after-effect of the leech bite.

The leeches lay still a moment. Then more confused writhing.

'Come on, come on . . .' Dylan muttered.

'Stand back a bit, I think they're smelling us,' said Dad.

Everyone stepped away. For a moment, the leeches quested uselessly.

Then, almost as one body, they inched hungrily to Tor's vial and began to climb the sides.

'Oh, thank the River,' said Firth. Dad said nothing, but hid his face a moment in both hands. Wordlessly, Dylan corked the third vial, and returned it to the tin. He returned the leeches to the jar, and took them back to the storeroom. He paused there to look at the dried-out hag that lived next to them on the shelf. It bared its circle of teeth at him, nothing but a round mouth where the head should be. It was small – to look at, much like an ordinary hagfish, except that it was a fleshy red-pink colour – but it was the strongest native spirit-eater.

He had thought before about seeking one out. At first, after he had injured the man, hag attacks had been a regular feature of his nightmares. But it might be worth the horror. A hag attack would leave Dylan with only his human self – not a shapeshifter any longer.

When he came back, Dad and Uncle Firth were muttering to each other, and stopped abruptly when he walked in.

'Dyl,' said Dad, after a slight pause. 'You couldn't help—'

'I *know*,' said Dylan. He was suddenly, unfairly, dizzily angry: he needed everyone to stop pretending this was all right, immediately. 'The whole salting *point* is that I can't help it. That's what I keep saying.' It had been so easy for everyone else to insist the problem had gone away: they didn't have to fight the urges, or endure the dreams or the missing memories, or live with whatever his sea-self decided to do.

'I know it's difficult,' said Dad, in his annoyingly pacifying way. 'When I was your age—'

'You'd got the hang of it. You know you had. And you had no one to teach you. I've had everything, everything you can teach me – I know all of it – and I'm still like this.'

'I'm sure, with time—'

'How are you sure?'

There was silence; Dad had no answer. In the end it was Uncle Firth who spoke, so softly and kindly it made Dylan want to throw something at him.

'Well, we can never be sure about anything, Dylan,' he said. 'But I think what your dad means is, we have plenty of reason to hope.'

'Oh, well, that's all right then,' said Dylan. 'Let's all just *hope* I don't kill anyone else.'

'Hang on, now – we don't know the girl's going to die,' said Dad.

Dylan didn't trust himself to reply. He turned for the door. The anger and horror he felt was almost as strong as a sea-urge, and he didn't know what he might say, if he stayed.

'Dyl, wait a minute –'

Dylan ignored him. He had never fought with his parents before, and he didn't want to start. He just wanted to be alone.

*

Dylan loved his room. It was small – or at least, the part tall enough to stand in was small; to either side, the roof sloped away sharply. But there was room for his bed, piled with seal skin pelts and blankets, and a chest of drawers beside it with a lamp on top.

He knelt on the bed, and looked out of the window. From here you could see the loch spread out below. It was puckered all over with gathering waves, pawing restlessly at the shore, reaching and reaching and reaching for the land.

It was hard to say exactly when his anger morphed into sadness. By the time Dad knocked on the door, he had already been crying for some time.

'Come in,' he said.

Dad came and sat on the bed beside him. They didn't speak about the argument; there was no need.

'I wish I could stay with you, Dyl,' said Dad. 'The journey's going to take a while now – I'll have to go by boat until I'm clear of the hunt. If the others weren't waiting . . .'

Dylan understood. Which didn't make it any easier. 'They'll go crazy with worry as it is,' he said. He wiped his face, and attempted a smile. 'Go on, sling across a sea. You should've left already.'

'I have been engaged in High Dithering,' said Dad solemnly. Then he put an arm around Dylan's shoulders. 'Firth practically shoo-d me up here to say goodbye. But I don't want to leave you.'

Dylan wasn't sure he had the energy to tell Dad to leave a second time, so he just concentrated on not asking him to stay, and not crying.

'You're a good person, Dylan,' said Dad.

He didn't trust himself to reply.

'It's hard being what we are,' he went on. 'It took all of us time to master it. But we're necessary. We're strong, but so are the threats at sea. It's a burden, and it's brave.'

'I'm not necessary. It's two for a Weard.'

'A formality,' said Dad dismissively. The Lore called for two, because with less than two there were some jobs you couldn't do; and presumably because there was a fear that too many would mean the Isles were overrun with wyrms. But none of the family took it particularly seriously, the formal division of their little band into Weard and mere weard-kin. It was understood that Dylan would dedicate his life to defending the Isles, regardless of title.

Still. It did mean he wasn't strictly necessary.

When he didn't reply, Dad squeezed him tighter. 'I think we owe you an apology,' he said. 'You tried to tell us how hard it still is for you, and maybe we didn't listen properly. You seemed in control . . .'

'But I have to fight for that control, all the time,' Dylan burst out. 'It hurts when I don't do what it wants. And I still don't remember the sea properly, and that scares me so much, every time . . .'

'Yes.' Dad's head nodded against the top of Dylan's. 'And you tried to tell us, and I'm sorry that we didn't take you more seriously. We wanted so badly for you to be fine that we made ourselves believe it.' He moved back a little to look Dylan in the eye, arm still round his shoulder. 'I'll be honest with you,' he said, 'I don't know exactly what we'll do next. Like you said, we've taught you what we already know. But I can promise you that from now on, we'll work it out together. We're in this with you. And I know you'll get it under control, and when you do the British Isles will be lucky to have such a strong wyrm on their shores.'

'Thanks,' said Dylan. Not because he believed this forecast. It was more a thanks for the arm around him, and the steadying warmth of another person. But then Dad sighed, and pulled away.

'Be good, stay safe,' he recited, 'keep away from the caves and the clootie well. And the water, while the landmen are hunting. If it rains, get Uncle Firth to lock the doors and keep the key.'

Dylan nodded. But he wasn't planning to keep these rules, this time. He would certainly stay out of the water, but he had every intention of going to the caves on the Black Isle, as soon as Dad was gone. The caves held stagnant water, and where there was stagnant water so close to the sea, there were likely to be hags. Spirit-eaters.

It never occurred to Dad to repeat his instructions, or extract promises. The family trusted each other. He just nodded, and said, 'I love you, smallest monster.'

'Love you too.'

Dad stood, but kept a hand on Dylan's shoulder, unwilling to let him go. Then he straightened up and looked out of the window at the rolling water; and he nodded, as though answering a call.

'I'll be on my way then. Back before you know it.'

When Dad had shut the door, Dylan listened as his footsteps retreated – down to the empty bedrooms, on down to the muffled world below, where the sound was lost. But he heard the thud of the front door, loud and clear.

Then it was quiet.

SPIRIT-EATERS

FROM *THE SEA AND ITS CITIZENS*, DRAFT MANUSCRIPT

Spirit can be eaten directly by specialised predators. These are long-lived creatures, capable of hibernating for extended spells without food, albeit in weakened forms. They are mostly found in the sea or around the coast. They appear in some landmen tales as dramatic bloodsuckers, witches bargaining for voices, and other fanciful guises; the reality, in comparison, is usually disappointing.

Small spirit-eaters, such as leeches and bone-worms, are merely pests, taking spirit from a single source: from blood, or bone, or breath. Larger spirit-eaters are more of a concern – especially for shapeshifters, their preferred prey.

The hag, for example, is a common spirit-eater found around the coast of Britain. With three bites, it can entirely consume a 'dormant' spirit, destroying the shapeshifter's second form. The effect on the health of the shifter is poorly understood.

5

Dad had taken the good boat; the second-best boat sputtered unhappily at Dylan all the way up Loch Ness and out into Loch Dochfour, along the River Ness and out to sea. He was easily able to give landman boats a wide berth, but nonetheless he stayed in the little boat's wheelhouse, wearing a sou'wester with the hood up, to avoid any awkward explanations. It was frustrating to have to travel by boat at all, when the water on all sides looked so inviting.

He brought her gently ashore on an ebbing tide, on the blush-pink sand of a small bay. It was his favourite, hemmed with great black rocks, and overlooked by red cliffs, which were coppered now with bracken. And up there among the bracken, the cave mouths waited.

He scanned the beach. It was empty. He scanned the rocks at sea for merfolk, the sick silvermen outcasts with infected flesh, who lived at sea and took a nosy interest in everything the Weard did. But the rocks were empty too. He was alone.

He stayed facing the sea, his back to the caves, and looked at the welt on his hand where the leech had bitten him. Just a blood-eater. He needed something stronger.

Dylan had wanted to do this years ago. He probably would have done it already, if the Lore on hags wasn't so frustratingly incomplete. It was a cardinal rule of the family not to feed anything you didn't understand. Once, Meriel had secretly tried to raise a tiny squid-like creature they had never seen before; it mutated overnight, grew to half the size of her bedroom, and covered her in ink that had made her sick for three months.

Well, he was going to have to break a rule. He knew that his sea-self would die, and that was all he needed to know.

He stood a minute, watching his little boat bob on the waves. He felt sick with sadness. He hated his sea-self, but he loved the sea – he had not realised, until now, just how much.

The Lore said that a complete hag attack required three bites, for blood and bone and breath. The first time Dylan had thought about doing this – after he had attacked the first man – it had given him recurring nightmares. But now that he was really going to do it, he found that his sadness was much greater than his fear.

His sea-self strained for the waves. *May the Sea keep your spirit*, he found himself thinking, by way of farewell. Which didn't even make any sense, under the circumstances.

Then he turned, plodded along the sand, and scrambled up the banks of thrift and marram grass to the most promisingly forbidden of the caves.

This one was long and thin, and ribbed like a gullet. At the very opening there was a patch of sunlight on the ground, cut sharply to the shape of the cave's mouth, imprinted now with Dylan's long shadow.

He had been this far before: he had sung rounds here for hours with Meriel and Tor when they were all smaller, just to hear their voices ring out strangely against the rock. Now he walked deeper in.

It narrowed uncomfortably, until he was hunching his shoulders in on both sides. He found himself singing again, to encourage himself – a lilting song about a selkie who had given up her seal form for her lover. It was a sad one. 'Hey, ho,' he sang – softly, but the cave made it ring – 'No more, no more, do I wish to wake at my silver shore . . .'

The sound lingered like mist. Dylan walked further into the dark, and both shoulders lightly grazed damp cave wall. 'My spirit I'll give, and I'll go to live with my love forever, ever more . . .'

Then the cave opened out – it was too dark to see now, but from the drips and splashes he could tell that there were little pools and puddles here; and on *ever more*, his voice suddenly magnified, carried up and out by the unseen architecture of the rock.

'On land, forever more,' he concluded, coming to a halt. The sound rang around him, mixed with the drip-dripping of the damp cave. There was a slight hissing too, of unseen water running through a fissure somewhere.

It seemed to him that the wish in his voice still lingered, even when the sound was gone. Then the wishing was gone too – and there was only the hissing, and the drip. The drip was forlorn, as though the water here was tired of its life, rising hopefully as vapour only to meet the cave roof again, and drip back down.

He should have brought matches. With one hand, he reached out for any kind of surface. His hand only met air.

The blackness pressed against him. Somehow, it seemed to make it harder to breathe.

He lifted a foot, and put it down very carefully. When he did the same with his other foot, it met something sloped and slippery, and he had to shuffle awkwardly to find an even surface, and ended up ankle deep in a puddle.

His heart was loud in his ears, and the hiss of water seemed louder too. Although, oddly, not the dripping. And then, with sudden certainty, he understood that it wasn't water hissing.

Horror took over. All purpose forgotten, he scrambled backwards, but there was a rock – maybe a stalagmite – he only knew he fell. The floor was damp and cold. The hissing seemed to fill the whole cave. It was impossible to see where the hag was, in the darkness.

He only knew for sure that it was close when he felt it on his throat.

It was small, muscular and damp. And strong – as it crossed his throat it squeezed, and it felt as though someone had stood on his windpipe. By the time he had recovered, the little rope of muscle had already inched across his shoulder and down his arm.

Dylan took a gulp of breath as his throat eased. All thought of letting this happen was gone: he was acting in blind panic. He took hold of the hag with his right hand, and pulled.

Too late – the hag bit into his wrist. He cried out in pain, and let go. The cave took his cry and threw it upwards and outwards, but there was no one to hear it.

Besides the gasping for breath and the pain in his wrist, something else was making his head ring - something like a sudden deafness. But it wasn't his human ears that had failed. It was some part of him that had always been listening to an elsewhere, and he had never even quite known it, and now it was gone.

The hag moved on. But to Dylan's horror, it left behind a strip of its own flesh, embedded in him and wrapped around his wrist. He scrabbled at it frantically. But there was no time – the hag had slipped under his jumper now, and was moving across his stomach, up to his chest. Blood from the wrist: bone from the ribs.

The breathlessness and pain were dizzying, but he forced himself to sit up. Tugging up his jumper, he grasped at the hag before it could take its second bite. He dug his fingers under it and pulled, and one end came, along with patches of his skin where it had clung tight. For a brief moment he thought it was over. Then the strip of flesh on his wrist contracted, squeezing him tightly, threatening to crush the bone until he gasped in pain and let the hag go. There was a damp *thwack* as it whipped itself back against his ribs, and bit into flesh.

After that, all his tugging couldn't pull it away. He knew when it had reached bone because something in him snapped, with a blinding pain; he clutched his side, expecting a physical break, but his human form was in one piece. And now the hag was inching up again – leaving another piece of flesh embedded in him – moving towards his throat. Blood, bone and breath.

He stood, and threw himself repeatedly against the cave wall, slamming the hag at the rock.

The hissing became a thin shriek of outrage, like metal on metal. It coiled out from the neck of his jumper, writhing, and fell down, but caught itself on the wool of his sleeve and hung on.

He dragged his shoulder along the wall to the narrow tunnel he had come in by, and squeezed through it, crushing his sides against the walls. At first the hag's flesh crushed his wrist in response, but he could feel it growing weaker. He stumbled towards the light, dragging it against the cave wall as he went, and at the cave mouth he pulled it, still shrieking, off the wool. He held it up, away from him.

It twisted and wheezed. Without his skin and blood to keep it going, it wouldn't live for long out of the water. It was hideous, a pulsing worm-like creature, no bigger than his hand, with a wide-open circular mouth of tiny needle teeth where there ought to be a head. It flailed.

It gnashed at his hand, and he dropped it into the marram grass. Then he pelted out of the cave, down the slope. He paused to look only once, at the foot of the slope; the thing wheezed and writhed horribly now, but it still inched determinedly towards him across the grasses. He turned and ran, staggering across the beach, not thinking at all, heading straight for the place where he was strong and safe and invincible.

The waves made him stumble, but even as he was pulled over, he knew it was just their motion and not the usual power dragging him down. His skin woke in the water, like a flower for the sun, but it stayed soft and small.

He crawled onwards nonetheless, first into the waves swelling and grabbing at each other, then into the swirling water underneath the waves' skin, until the seabed sloped sharply and he reached the still water of the world below.

He didn't drown. His skin still breathed. But he didn't transform.

He hung suspended in the sea, and willed his mind to focus.

In the water, his body didn't hurt anymore. He let himself drift down to the seabed, and waited there for his heart to slow.

The sea felt vast.

He held up a hand. A human hand. A butterfish drifted past, and it was *bigger* than his hand. He could see its round silver eye, the neat soldierly fins, and it was mesmerising – before, fish had just been dots flickering past him, like flies on land.

Dreamlike, he kicked off from the sand and followed this newly magnified fish. It flicked at once into a higher gear, and outpaced him easily. For a minute he chased it, willing his little body to accelerate, but the seascape just kept drifting by in its new huge slowness. It didn't help that he was still dressed in wool and linen, filling with water, weighing him down.

He gave in, and drifted back down to the seabed. There was seagrass here, a meadow, which once had only tickled his belly; he knelt in it now. Herring fingerlings swarmed out from beneath him, flashing out and back into the safety of the grasses.

He was still an ocean creature. But his other body was gone – he was like a silverman now, albeit impervious to salt. It was a partial transformation: the two pieces of flesh were feeding on him, but the hag hadn't finished the job.

He had done it on purpose. That thought seemed a very, very long way away – a thought that belonged on the land, to a boy who had never known the horror of that cave.

He felt the tell-tale tightening of the flesh against his wrist and ribs before he saw the hag, curled in a ball, spinning and rolling across the seafloor toward him with uncanny speed. Instinctually, he brought up his hands full of mud and sand and flung them at the wheeling hag, which recoiled a moment in a murky cloud. He didn't wait: he was gone, slicing through the water for the shore as fast as his little body could carry him.

He didn't stop or look back until he was crawling through breaking waves, then foam, then stumbling upright on to the heavy sand of the shoreline, still not stopping until there was enough good dry land between him and his watery hunter, and the tightness against his wrist and ribs slackened and cooled. Then he stopped, and fell to his knees, and gasped for breath.

It had been stupid to linger in the sea, where the thing could breathe, and give chase. For several long minutes he stayed where he was. Now that the dreamlike ocean was behind him, all his old thoughts were crowding back in. He had wanted this – he had attacked someone – two people. Why had he run away? He stood and looked at the sea, and experimented with the idea of returning – of dragging himself back out there, and letting the hag take his throat. Then it would be finished.

He didn't know how long it was before he turned away.

He hugged his bloodied arms to himself, his soaked clothes dragging at his skin. Then he walked back to his boat. It was over.

SEA-SILVER

FROM *THE SEA AND ITS CITIZENS*, DRAFT MANUSCRIPT

Sea-silver is harvested from vents in the seafloor, where the earth cracks and its hidden metals seep into the ocean.

It has the same uses as ordinary silver: it weakens water creatures, and may therefore be used as a defensive ward, a weapon, a binding, or to remove barbs and parasites left in flesh. It is, however, much more powerful than ordinary silver.

Despite calls for revision, it is still against the River Lore to keep sea-silver on a silverman boat. This is a useless superstition, stemming from a general refusal to engage with the sea in any form. For the Sea Weard, a supply of this potent silver is essential; in most cases, there is no substitute.

6

The landman boats had gone home. The empty loch was as smooth as spilt ink, split by a single furrow in the wake of Dylan's boat; in the low light, the surrounding hills were marbled in gold and green and shadow. Dylan was used to travelling below the water. Up here on the surface, in his human skin, he felt very small.

He moored, and walked up shingle and into pine-shadows, towards the cottage. His skin seemed to be getting colder as it dried – and the bones beneath too, as though the water had seeped inside. There was a dull throb at his wrist and rib, but it was his other cuts and bruises that hurt him the most now.

With the cottage in sight, he hesitated.

He would have to explain what he'd done. First to Uncle Firth; soon, to everyone.

He might have kept walking if that was his only fear, but there was another, and it was worse. There might be news of the girl. So he stood, looking at the cottage.

In the end, it was the bone-cold that pushed him forwards. It would be warm inside, and he could eat – he was ravenous – a little faint too, he realised dimly. He only noticed the kelpie when he was at the door. It sat below the window in human form, cross-legged and sulky.

'Dylan Pade,' it said.

Dylan didn't bother to reply. He opened the cottage door. Inside, a fire was crackling in the grate, and as the warmth of home enveloped him, he let out a small keening sound of relief.

At the sound of the door, Uncle Firth looked up from his armchair, all cheery delight – until he saw Dylan. His face fell.

'Dylan! What happened?'

Dylan was still reeling from the warm-and-home feeling; it brought the horror and the fear with it, redoubled, now that he was somewhere safe to feel it all. Answering his uncle's question seemed unfathomably difficult. He considered trying, but gave in, and tottered to an armchair.

Uncle Firth opened his mouth to ask a second time – then, in response to Dylan's pleading eyes, he shut it again. He went instead to the kitchen, and returned with the medicine tin and a large bar of landman chocolate. He had his silverman-in-a-crisis face on: practical, calm, orderly.

'Here,' he said, handing Dylan the chocolate. 'Eat. I'll get you cleaned up.' His eyes roved over Dylan's bloodied face and torn up jumper. 'Any hidden injuries I should know about?'

Dylan thought about the hagflesh – but he shook his head. He dutifully bit into the chocolate, as his uncle rummaged through the tin, and produced sage balm for Dylan's face. He began to dab. It stung.

'Sorry,' he said, when Dylan flinched. 'Keep eating that chocolate, you're pale as merfolk. When I'm done here, I'll want to know what happened.' He tilted Dylan's face a little, and dabbed again. 'But first,' he said, 'I have some good news for you. I went down to the shore earlier, when the landmen were taking a break. The girl pulled through the worst of it. The doctor says she'll live.' He inspected Dylan's face: 'Turn left a little – river, that's nasty – hey, now. No crying on my sage balm. You're making it all runny.' But he was smiling as he said it, and he squeezed Dylan's shoulder, in an awkward little gesture of understanding. His own eyes were shining with answering tears. 'I'm so glad, Dylan,' he said. 'So glad.'

'Thank you for finding out.'

'Of course,' he said; and he went back to daubing Dylan's face, and they didn't speak again until he had finished. Dylan could not have found the words. He was not a murderer. And he never would be, now. He was free. Every moment of terror in that cave suddenly seemed worth it. The warmth of the fire was wonderful on his human skin. Even the sting of sage balm on human wounds felt like a blessing.

Outside, slow, fat raindrops began to drip down the windowpane. Nothing inside him roared. It was over.

Uncle Firth finished with Dylan's face, and went to roll up his jumper sleeve. Dylan flinched away. His uncle looked quizzical: it was time to explain.

'I need to tell you what happened first,' said Dylan.

'All right . . .' Uncle Firth rocked back on his heels, in the silvermen's favourite position, a comfortable squat. He looked up at Dylan, all kind concern. Dylan had no idea how he would take this.

'Do you know what a sea hag is?' he said.

From the look on his uncle's face, it was very clear that he did. Not many silvermen cared to know any Sea Lore, but Uncle Firth was different.

'Right. So. That's what happened – a hag. It bit me twice.' Dylan rolled up his sleeve. He hadn't actually looked at the strips of flesh since the attack. This one was blood red and pulsing slightly; around it, his own skin was broken and weeping. It looked much worse than it felt.

'River and *moon*,' said Uncle Firth, standing. 'I'll get the sea-silver . . .'

'We don't have any,' said Dylan. 'The others took the last.'

Uncle Firth made a very visible effort not to panic, nodding far too many times, and running a hand through his already-upright hair. 'Right. Right. Then we'll have to get on a train to your grandpa. He'll be at the docks in London for the Way. He might have some . . .'

This was not a bad idea. Grandpa Willig was a highly unorthodox silverman healer, and probably not above keeping illicit sea-silver on his boat. And the week after Equinox was one of the few times you could be sure where he was, as he always joined the Way, the group of scholars crossing the Rivers Avon and Thames from west to east. But Dylan shook his head.

'I don't want sea-silver,' he said.

'Silver will kill off those bits of hag.' Uncle Firth said this kindly, as though he thought Dylan's brain must have got addled. 'They're eating your sea-spirit, aren't they? We need to get them out. I'll get the train timetable.'

'No – it wasn't –' Dylan tried; then, 'I don't . . .' And

finally, 'I did it on purpose. I don't want to save my sea-self. I don't want it back.'

For a moment, Uncle Firth looked at him as though he hadn't spoken English. Then, slowly, comprehension dawned.

'Oh, *Dylan*.'

'I know, I know it was risky. And it was awful. But it's worked! And it only got me twice, so I can still go in the sea. I just don't transform.' It struck him for the first time how wonderful this was. 'I'm like you! Only, salt water's fine. And really, I know it looks bad, but it hardly hurts.'

'But it's eating you? Right now?' said Uncle Firth.

'My sea-self, yes.' Dylan tried to find a way to explain this without upsetting his uncle more. 'People are always producing spirit, so it latches on and keeps eating as I make more. It's not like – I won't get worse. It would need a third bite to finish my sea-self off.'

'Right.'

'It only eats the dormant spirit,' said Dylan. 'I can't even feel it happening, in my human form.'

Uncle Firth was trying, and failing, to regain his calm-and-orderly face. 'And – side effects?' he asked.

Dylan considered blurring the truth here – he knew Uncle Firth did not deal well with uncertainty – but he wasn't a natural liar. 'I don't know. A lot of the Lore is missing. But so far it's fine.'

If Uncle Firth knew how to be angry, Dylan had never seen it. Instead, he stared at Dylan now with a panicked disbelief that made him look childlike – as though Dylan was, out of nowhere, kicking him repeatedly. 'Dylan. Those things are dangerous. It's eating half your spirit! We have no idea if you can survive that . . .'

'I feel fine . . .'

'For now. That tells us almost nothing. This is . . . we have to go and see your grandpa . . .'

'I don't want—'

'Salting tides, Dylan, what if it kills you?'

They stared at each other, uncle and nephew: so alike to look at, but living such impossibly different lives. 'You don't know what it's like,' Dylan said at last – and even to his own ears it sounded petulant, childish. But it was true. 'There's a whole half of my life I can't control. And it takes over the other half . . . Sometimes I try and imagine what the rest of my life is going to be like and all I can ever think is, *Won't it be great if I never kill anyone.*'

Uncle Firth had no reply; just more hand-through-hair business.

'Everyone says I'm so necessary,' Dylan went on, warming to his theme, 'but the Lore says you need two in a Weard. We've got Mam and Dad, and after that it'll be Meriel and Tor – I'm just a spare. It's pointless. I could be normal. I could . . .' And Dylan gestured wildly, as though a wave of his hands could indicate all the things that other people just assumed would happen to them, which he had never been allowed to even contemplate. But of course, it couldn't. He concluded, rather lamely: 'I don't want to be a wyrm.'

Uncle Firth shook his head. 'I understand. But—'

'No,' said Dylan. He wasn't trying to be argumentative – he was just full of sudden clarity, like the first light of dawn inside him. 'You *don't* understand. I've made my decision. I did this on purpose. And I'm not undoing it.'

'Your parents –'

Dylan didn't want to think about his parents. He stood. 'I'm going outside,' he said. 'I've never felt the rain on my skin before – not properly – the other me was always in the way.' He looked at his uncle, but he seemed small, and distant – everything felt strange, in this new clear shining world. Still, he hadn't meant to upset Uncle Firth. 'I'm sorry,' he said,

Then he walked to the door, and stepped outside, and felt soft quiet rain on his skin, and calm.

A dove-grey dusk had fallen by the time Uncle Firth came outside. Dylan was sitting under the eaves, palms out to feel the half-hearted rain. The kelpie was off among the trees being a dismal horse; below them, the loch was turning black.

Uncle Firth sat down beside Dylan in a squat.

'You're right,' he said, after a moment. 'I can't understand anything about the sea, or having more than one shape.'

'Sorry for being rude,' said Dylan.

'No – don't bother with that. This is about the decisions that will determine your whole life. It's not about politeness.'

Dylan nodded.

'But I do understand,' Uncle Firth went on, 'about guilt. As you know.'

Dylan nodded again. It made him desperately sorry for Uncle Firth, the story of him and Auntie Isla. They rarely spoke of it, but he thought of it sometimes when he watched his uncle in some particularly gentle and self-effacing act – he moved through the world like someone always afraid of breaking it.

'So,' Uncle Firth went on, 'I know guilt – and the fear of more guilt – and I don't underestimate it. It hurts. Physically. And it's relentless.'

Dylan leaned his head back against the cottage wall. 'You're not even allowed to try and feel better,' he said, 'because you don't have the right.'

His uncle nodded. 'It can feel that way, certainly.' And for a moment, they both just sat, and felt the rain.

'I'm not going to tell you how you should live your life,' said Uncle Firth. 'But. You are my nephew. You have just been bitten by a dangerous and largely unknown spirit-eater. We don't know what it will do.'

Dylan just nodded again, tensing for what was to come.

'So here's what I propose,' said Uncle Firth. 'We will get the morning train to London tomorrow. We will find out if Grandpa Willig has sea-silver.' Dylan began to protest, but Uncle Firth kept talking. 'And,' he said, 'if he does, I will not force it on you. If you don't want your sea-self back, that's your choice to make. For as long as you feel well, you can take this risk, and stay as you are – at least until your parents get back – I don't know what they'll have to say about it. But I don't want you waking in the middle of the night with a raging fever, and deciding at that point that maybe it would have been good to have some sea-silver on hand after all.'

Dylan had to concede that this was reasonable. It slightly

marred his light, free feeling. But it was practical. And a child of the Weard knew how to be practical.

'Yes,' he said. 'All right.'

'Good,' said Uncle Firth. Then, 'I've made trout stew.'

'Thank you,' said Dylan earnestly.

Uncle Firth stood, and held out a hand to help Dylan up. Below, the quiet of the evening was torn by a flock of geese, launching into the sky, calling to each other to leave the loch behind and fly home for the approaching night.

'Come inside then,' said Uncle Firth. 'Let's eat.'

Uncle Firth made excellent stews. They ate at the fireside, sitting in the armchairs. Dylan felt wonderfully warm and full. Besides a dull ache at his wrist and ribs, he seemed completely well – battered and tired, but well. Rain fell on the roof, and nothing stirred inside him, and it was an astonishingly safe feeling.

When they had eaten, they both read for a while by the fire. The evening wore on, and Uncle Firth did not suggest they go to bed. Dylan suspected he was unwilling to part ways for the night, in case his nephew suddenly began flailing or frothing at the mouth or something, out of his sight.

'I'll clear up,' suggested Dylan at last, when he was too tired to focus on a complete sentence.

'Yes,' said Uncle Firth reluctantly – but yawning. 'It might be time.' And he stood, and picked up his and Dylan's bowls. Dylan went to clear the table, still strewn with the mess of the day. It felt like a lifetime ago that they had watched the leeches, waiting to see if Mam and Meriel and Tor were alive.

He scooped up the books, then went to pick up Tor's vial of blood. Then he stopped.

The blood inside was a dark, ugly shade of maroon, and it was churning and frothing, tugged in intricate miniature currents around the vials. Dylan's gut squeezed horribly. He opened the tin and looked at the other vials: Mam's, Meriel's, Dad's. Everybody's blood looked the same.

His own vial was frothing too, but that was unsurprising; he was being consumed by a hag right now. He had only ever seen the fizz of a leech bite before now, but he knew what restless blood meant. A spirit-eater.

The family had been attacked by a spirit-eater, somewhere at sea. They needed help. And Dylan was horribly, uselessly human.

NÁLS

FROM *THE SEA AND ITS CITIZENS*, DRAFT MANUSCRIPT

A nál is a particularly ancient and powerful form of spirit-eater. They are poorly understood, as the few living examples have been bound for many centuries now. Wyrms from around the world contribute to their continued re-binding.

Their bound form is a sea-serpent, but at full strength they are also a sea-current. As a sea-current, they may peel off pieces of themselves into smaller threads of current that reel in, trap and feed on prey.

Unlike many spirit-eaters, they are not restricted to feeding on dormant spirit. They will feed on anything alive, and kill it in the process.

7

Dylan couldn't sleep that night. He sat downstairs at the table in a pool of lamplight, wrapped in his blanket. He no longer even noticed the miracle of the rain on the roof.

He and Uncle Firth had talked it over, and after half-heartedly attempting a balm made with ordinary silver, they had agreed that there was nothing to do but see Grandpa Willig as planned. Dylan wanted to wade into the loch and out to sea right away, but he wouldn't be strong enough in this form to fight off anything feasting on his family, or carry anyone wounded home – if he even survived the journey there in the first place. And if they weren't in the Sargasso Sea with the nál, it would take him forever to search for them while he was this size.

There were plenty of other spirit-eaters at sea; it might not be the nál. This thought preoccupied him, as he stared at the guttering flame. If he could only know for sure what was happening to them, then his mind wouldn't fill with every possible awful fate . . .

He was jerked out of his reverie by something nudging at

the window. He looked up, and saw the shadowy outline of a horse.

He stood, strode to the window and opened it, blanket flapping like a cloak. Cold damp air rushed in – but, he realised, it had stopped raining. 'What?' he said. 'What do you want? Do you know what's attacked them?'

But the kelpie just carried on being a horse.

'Wait there,' said Dylan – and he went and fetched a vial of blood. He took it to the window. 'Do you know what this means? Is it the nál?'

If anything, the kelpie was even more emphatically a horse.

Dylan sagged. '*Fine*,' he said, and slammed the window shut.

Some of the cold air lingered, and he was more alert now, and restless. He wandered to the windows at the front of the house, facing towards the loch. There was, he saw, the faintest hint of grey light in the dark sky: dawn was on its way. The ebb tide would peak soon – a full tidal cycle since he had stupidly given himself to the hag.

He realised that he couldn't feel the tide tugging anymore. He used to know when it was turning, as clearly as he knew when the sun was rising. It was a peculiar kind of silence, not feeling the colossal shift of all the world's water, which dragged whole currents around as it turned – the coastal currents of Britain flipped themselves over into their own mirror image, twice a day. Merfolk used them to slip up and down the Isles at speed.

Dylan was on his feet before he consciously registered that he'd had an idea. The eastern ebb current flowed south to north. If you wanted to find the merfolk in northern waters, the peak of the ebb tide was the ideal time.

In three long strides Dylan was at the door; then he slid back the lock and was out in the bitter morning, hurrying through the pines in the almost-darkness.

Mostly, no one *did* want to find the folk. They were silvermen sickened by an eel-bite, without ever reaching the wyrm-state of Mam and Dad: instead, the sickness merely caused parts of their flesh to wither into dark fish-like stumps, and soured their blood to suit sea water. Exiled from the other silvermen, they were insular and proud, keeping everyone else at a distance. But they knew the signs of the sea. A nál could distort ocean currents for miles, and if one was now dangerously unbound the folk would know, even at this distance. And they respected the Weard enough to tell Dylan what they knew. Probably.

He hurried through trees to shingle. When he reached the shore, he kept walking without hesitation into the shocking cold of the loch. No power overcame him. It was peculiar, like jumping and failing to fall. Weightless, he waded out up to his waist, marvelling at the oddity of being half in the air and half in the water. Then he kicked off against the sand, and slipped under the surface.

It was the most familiar journey in his world: through Loch Ness and Loch Dochfour to the River Ness, on out into the sea. But it was different now. The peat-filled water felt heavy, and when he struck out into the middle of the loch, he was suddenly aware of its cavernous depth. He paused, amazed, suspended in the darkness like a star.

Then he spun his small body in a loop-de-loop, barely rippling the water around him, and set off, slipping through the blackness to the sea.

The journey took much longer in his new form, although thankfully he was not as slow as landmen. He moved like a silverman now. By the time he reached the clear water of the river, shafts of morning light were cutting through the current, winking on the pebbles below. The salt tang of the sea began here, and the pulse of waves, although the pulsing grew weaker as time passed. The tide was ebbing fast.

At the frenzied rush of water where river met sea, Dylan veered north, into a sheltered firth. Here, the merfolk had one of their nests.

'Nests' is what the Pades called them; presumably, the folk themselves called them something more dignified. He hoped some of them would be there. Merfolk were still silvermen at heart, and couldn't bear a fixed abode. They travelled swiftly on coastal currents. Around the Isles, they kept safe havens in secluded bays and firths and inlets – seas where they could spend the night, and rest.

The water in the firth was restless today, scattering silt, and giving the sea a thick green complexion. Dylan couldn't see far ahead. He dropped close to the seafloor so that he wouldn't miss the nest, his belly skimming kelp and crabs and starfish. He followed the bed as it sloped steeply downwards, and changed from sand and shell to thick mud. He was close.

He only spotted the first furrow when he was swimming right over it.

It was a deep, slender groove in the mud, perfectly shaped

to somebody's particular body, and lined with soft grasses. Its owner could sleep in there, sheltered from the incessant rolling of the water. But right now, it was empty.

Dylan snaked along the line of furrows, then out around them in ever-growing circles. He saw the smaller signs of merfolk, the signs that you could so easily mistake for more seabed debris if you weren't paying attention: the half-buried shell-jars and tools, sunk into the mud for safe-keeping; the circle of stones that marked out their gathering place; further out still, the vicious spikes of silver wards to strengthen the water and deter its smaller predators. When Dylan had completed a loop of the silver, there was nowhere else to look. The nest was empty.

They might yet be somewhere else in the firth, he supposed. Or they might arrive later. He could linger a little, but he had to be back for the train soon . . .

A sudden disturbance of the water made him swing round in alarm. For a moment, there was too much silt and swirling foam to see. Then he made out the figure in the water: a man, his body partially scaled. Merfolk.

Dylan's heart leaped. He knew very little of the merfolk's signed language, but he held his arms out with palms open in their customary greeting.

The man responded in kind. Dylan couldn't make his face out clearly, but something seemed to alarm him – which made Dylan glance instinctually over his shoulder, but there was nothing there. Then he gave another signal Dylan knew, because it was an easy one: *up*.

The two of them swam for the surface and a little inland,

the man leading. They swam up towards the marbled light, and the flat pebbles of air puckering the surface; then they burst through into foam and waves.

The man had brought them to a cluster of rocks, and he heaved himself up in a single swing. Dylan followed, rather inelegantly. His human arms were weak, and his palms tore on the crust of barnacles. But at last he was up, and they could talk.

The man spoke first, before Dylan could gather his thoughts. He pointed at the flesh around Dylan's wrist. 'You have been attacked?'

'Yes,' said Dylan – shouting a little over the crash of waves. 'Two bites.' He realised, now, that the man was very young – somewhere between boyhood and manhood. Like all merfolk, he was pale: Dylan didn't know if it was the sickness, or the lack of sunlight. Probably both. He had a silverman's grey eyes, but his fair hair was crusted with salt. The disease had taken him entirely from the waist down, in a neat division between healthy flesh and scaled, fused legs; with a fan of scales at the end, he almost looked like the pictures you found in landman tales.

The boy's grey eyes were wide with alarm. 'You are not safe here,' he said, 'Child of the Weard.'

'What? Why?'

The boy pointed again at the flesh. 'The hag seeks its third bite.'

Dylan had forgotten how annoyingly formal and mysterious the folk were. 'Yes, but . . .' – he gestured at the vast sea all around them, trying to convey the madness of one tiny predator seeking one tiny bite of prey in all that water. 'I don't think it's likely to find me,' he said.

The boy looked at Dylan with head cocked; he seemed as fascinated by Dylan, in his own way, as Dylan was by him. 'You do not know?' he said. He reached out, and gently touched the flesh. 'It has left itself in you. It feels you now, as a homing bird feels the north. It can always find you.'

Dylan stared at him. The waves pounded the rock. Overhead, a gull cried.

'It is one of the fastest creatures of the water,' the boy said. 'It must be asleep, or it would already have found you here – and if it had taken its last bite in the sea, you would have drowned. You are fortunate, child of the Weard. Sea-silver would restore you –'

'I don't have any,' said Dylan. He didn't *feel* fortunate. 'And there's no one left to get some. My family are gone, and something's hurting them . . .'

'The Weard are hurt?' said the boy. 'How do you know this?'

Dylan hollered an explanation about the blood, while panic twisted his gut. If he couldn't go in the water at all, what was he supposed to do if he couldn't find silver? Wait at home, leaving them all to die? Live there alone for the rest of his life, with the guilt and the silence?

Like an echo of his thoughts, the boy asked, 'What will you do?'

'I'm getting a train to see my grandpa,' said Dylan. This much, at least, was clear. 'He's doing the Way this year, so we can find him in London. He might have sea-silver. Once I've got my sea-self back, I'll go after the others.'

The boy nodded. 'This is good,' he said. 'You must make haste. We have seen signs in the sea: the currents are beginning to bend, and creatures of the south-west are fleeing here to the north. We had suspected the nál was unbound. If it has the Weard, this is grave news.'

Dylan was surprised by how calmly he received this information. He had already believed this, really. He had known it since he saw the fizzing churn of the blood.

'That's what I came to ask,' he said flatly.

'We must assume it also has the wyrms of other shores, if your family are not freed soon,' said the boy thoughtfully. 'If they were at liberty, they would bind it.'

'Yes,' agreed Dylan dismally.

'I shall tell the others at the morning watching hour. If your grandfather does not have silver, perhaps we may find another way.'

Dylan had murky memories of seeing the lamps the merfolk used at watching hour, in the dark layer of the sea where the daylight first began to fail. Messages were flashed out with their merlights, the nearest bright white like stars, their distant echoes fading to blue.

It was a kindness for one of the merfolk to volunteer help unasked. 'Thank you,' said Dylan earnestly. He looked up at the sun, beginning its westward drift. 'I should go. I have to be back for the train.'

'You must walk. The water is not safe.'

Dylan shook his head, still not quite able to believe this. 'That would take all day. I'll miss the train. I have to get to London, today – there's not time . . .'

'The water is not safe,' the boy repeated. 'But – haste is advisable.' He considered, his face taking on the practical silverman look that Dylan knew so well; it made him look, suddenly, far more human. 'I will travel with you,' he said. 'We will swim close to the shore. If the hag attacks, strike for the shore, and I will defend you.'

From one of the merfolk, this was an extraordinary offer. Dylan knew they respected the Weard, but he had never heard one volunteer to act as a personal guard before. 'Thank you,' he said fervently.

The boy only bowed his head slightly, looking uneasy. He would not have been thanked by anyone since he left the silvermen; it wasn't the folk way. Dylan wondered how old he had been when he was bitten. Did his family ever come to the peace moorings to see him? Or were they old-school purists, the type who still thought anyone infected ought to be killed?

The boy looked at Dylan's wrist, and Dylan saw a mirror of his own thoughts – sympathetic, curious. 'How did it find you?' he asked.

It didn't occur to Dylan to lie. Perhaps he liked this boy instinctually, or perhaps it was desperation that made his heart reach out for a friend, any friend, on that rock in the middle of the sea. 'I went looking for it,' he said. 'I can't control my sea-self. I was trying to kill it.'

The boy's sympathetic look softened even further, but he shook his head. 'Spirit is never destroyed,' he said. 'Only transferred. This hag will grow in power now.' Dylan knew how spirit-eating worked, and still felt that this came to much the same thing: his sea-self was still gone. But he didn't have the heart to debate the point. Besides, the boy was distracted, scanning the criss-cross wrinkles on the surface of the waves for any danger signals. 'We should go,' he said. 'The longer we wait, the greater the chance it will wake.'

'Right,' said Dylan. 'Thank you. Again. It's very generous of you.'

The boy hesitated a moment, then said, 'It is not. Your family have meant more to me than you know.' And before Dylan could say anything to this, the boy firmly ended their talk by holding a fist to his chest, head bowed. 'Child of the Weard,' he said.

Dylan wanted to ask questions, but the boy's eyes were firmly cast down, and he knew better than to push his luck. It was not unusual for other citizens of the Sea to be personally indebted to the Weard for fighting some predator, especially in the coastal waters. He felt a swell of sad pride at this reminder of how necessary, how valuable, his family were.

'I'm Dylan,' he said. 'Please call me Dylan. What's your name?'

The boy raised his head. For a moment there was a sudden hunger in his eyes, and Dylan wondered again when he had been exiled, and how long it had been since conversation was free and easy and warm.

'Dylan,' he said, nodding. 'My name is Caspian.'

RELATIONS BETWEEN SILVERMEN AND OUR SEA COUSINS
FROM *THE SEA AND ITS CITIZENS*, DRAFT MANUSCRIPT

The history of the relations between silvermen, merfolk and the Weard is shameful.

The link between the folk and the Weard has only recently been appreciated. It has long been understood that an infected eel bite causes the mersickness, turning infected flesh scaled and limp. The medicine to halt this process has been known and administered for centuries, obscuring the fact that without treatment, the sickness will either kill the victim *or produce a wyrm*. This is because the bite is, in fact, a transference of spirit via blood.

Both mersickness and wyrms have historically been feared. Throughout recorded history, the mersick have been thrown overboard to die; even when treatment was discovered, this rule was still applied to anybody who lost too much of their flesh to the disease. In the twelfth century, silvermen killed the existing wyrms and outlawed the Sea Weard (ineffectually – thankfully, more wyrms arose and continued the work in secret). Both these positions have now been revised, but neither wyrms nor the mersick are made welcome on the river, and prejudice is still strong.

8

In light of Caspian's warnings, Dylan and Uncle Firth travelled above the water, taking the second-best boat to Inverness. On the train to London, Dylan slept at last. He woke to find the world outside was a blur of neat, hedge-hemmed fields in soft greens: England. Rain smeared the view. Dylan had slept, peacefully, through rain.

He watched the droplets chase each other down the glass. No one had told him rain could be like this – so cosy and quiet. But then, who could have told him? None of his family knew.

He looked over at Uncle Firth, who was lost in his own thoughts, looking out of the window. Somewhere in the folds of the hills they were tearing through, a river would be hiding. Dylan wondered if his uncle had missed this place, the way he himself already missed the wide-open light of home.

They hurried on, into dusk. The fields gave way to steep banks of grass below rows of thin houses, which marched onwards into London. Electric lights drowned the stars. Dylan felt very far from home.

*

It was an hour's walk from the station to reach St Katharine's Dock, where the silvermen would be moored. Dylan had seen London twice before, but it was just as shocking this time – full of noise and bustle, even at night. It was a relief to reach the quiet black water of the dock.

Uncle Firth knelt eagerly at the water's edge to splash his parched skin. It occurred to Dylan that he could do the same, now, without incident; but it felt wrong, so he stayed back, and waited for his uncle to finish.

The silverman boats were easy enough to identify, with their smaller rowboats fastened to their sides, and the silver chain alongside each mooring rope. And there in the middle, light spilling out around the blinds, was Grandpa Willig's blue boat.

Half a lifetime ago, this boat had been one of Dylan's favourite places in the world. Then it had been explained to him that his sea-self was now too big, and he couldn't be around the people on the rivers anymore, and wouldn't visit the blue boat again. Grandpa Willig had kept visiting the cottage, and over time, Dylan had slowly stopped feeling the sharp shard of hurt when he thought of the boat. To see it again made him feel suddenly very young, and much too tall.

They climbed aboard, and the creaky plank on the deck still creaked. They went to the door, and the old-fashioned lantern above it still swayed gently with the slight motion of the water. Uncle Firth knocked.

The door opened, and there was Grandpa Willig: small and portly, with a puff of white hair, and a round excitable face that usually smiled in just the same all-over way as Dad's.

But now, his expression was grave. He didn't seem surprised to see them. He pulled Uncle Firth at once into an embrace, then ushered him inside, and gave Dylan the same tight squeeze.

'My dear boy,' he whispered, redoubling the squeeze.

Did he already know?

It occurred to Dylan, for the first time, that Grandpa Willig's only son was lost at sea.

Then Grandpa released him from the hug and ushered him inside, and all thoughts of Grandpa's sorrows were driven from his mind.

The boat was crowded with people, all dressed in clothes made – if you looked closely – from waterproof caddisfly-silk: the uniform of silvermen. Designs ranged from old-fashioned one-piece suits, to the more stylish cuts that almost aped landman fashions; but even dressed in the new style, Dylan could always pick our silvermen from the unusual grey shade of their eyes. It was the same as his family's eyes.

Grandpa's galley table had been pushed to one end, and the dozen or so men and women inside had formed a very squashed circle, sitting on stools and benches and squatting on the floor. One of Grandpa's lamps had been placed in the centre – a speaker light, for a chittering. Dylan had never seen one of the formal silverman meetings, but Mam and Dad had talked about them.

'The merfolk have been,' said Grandpa. 'They've told us. Emergency chittering' – he flapped a hand at the other men and women. Two of the nearest silvermen shuffled over on a bench to make more room. Dylan sat; Uncle Firth squatted on the floor beside them, and frowned up at Willig.

'Merfolk?' he said. 'Here?'

'Well, just one in the docks, had to be inconspicuous – came to fetch us out to the peace moorings to talk with a group of them.'

'It's not like them, to seek us out,' said Uncle Firth.

'Ah well,' said Grandpa Willig – not sitting, but hovering at the edges of the circle, fingertips pressed together in his habitual way. 'Urgent business.' And Dylan silently thanked Caspian, and the ingenious merlights.

'Urgent *Sea* business,' said a lean man at the far side of the circle, seated on a stool. 'Not ours. They shouldn't have come.'

'We don't rule the folk, Merlin,' said a woman mildly. 'They can do what they like.'

'It's not River business. We shouldn't be getting involved.'

'It will be the River's business soon enough,' snapped another woman, 'if we leave the Sea unguarded. We need a Weard, Merlin, whatever you might personally feel –'

'We've already voted on this,' said the mild woman. 'It's the next lamp now.'

Dylan sat awkwardly half-on, half-off the bench, trying to be still and inconspicuous. He had never in his life shared a space with so many people – certainly never so many strangers. And it didn't exactly put him at ease to know that the importance of his family's lives had just been put to a vote. It was easy enough to pick out those who had agreed with Merlin. They had the studiously blank eyes and folded bodies of people who have lost an argument, and have now retreated, preparing to observe the ensuing stupidity and carry on being privately right.

Throughout this exchange, Grandpa Willig had not sat down. He remained standing, tense, ready to leap into action – any action – to do anything at all but stay still. He opened his mouth to speak again now, but another man put a hand on his arm to interrupt.

'It's been a long journey for the boys,' he said, nodding at Uncle Firth and Dylan. 'Shall I cook up some dinner?'

'Yes – of course – yes. Thank you, Trent. I've got chara cakes' – he wafted a hand towards the shelves by the stove. Trent nodded.

'You carry on,' he said. 'I'll fry.'

Grandpa Willig looked at Dylan. 'So. Ah – Dylan – are you able to – it would be good to hear, in your own words, what exactly – there were some facts the folk didn't have, and we have had to surmise. But if you're in need of a rest . . .'

'It's all right, Grandpa,' said Dylan. 'I'm fine.' He didn't feel like telling the story of his hag attack and his missing family to this grave-faced room of strangers – but that was not because of his tiredness or his hunger, and he might as well get it over with. But he might, he thought, leave out the part about doing it on purpose.

'Well, then – perhaps a lamp . . . ?' said Grandpa Willig, looking at the mild woman. The woman nodded, stood, and snuffed out the lamp at the centre of the circle, before lighting it again.

'Dylan Pade,' she announced. Everyone looked at him expectantly.

'Er,' said Dylan.

And everyone carried on looking at him expectantly. So, haltingly, he began.

He had a feeling the representative of the Weard ought to speak well, and that he was not speaking well at all. But everyone listened quietly to the end. Dylan was used to his family, where everyone would jump in talking at once if you left the smallest silence. Here he ground slowly to a halt, and still everyone waited, politely observing some etiquette that he only half understood.

'So, um,' he said, when he had told everything, and still no one jumped in to speak. 'Do you have sea-silver, Grandpa?'

'No,' said Grandpa Willig.

'Oh.' Dylan did not want to cry; but he was discovering that not-wanting-to-cry in front of a dozen other people is a muddling, hot feeling that, in itself, sort of makes you want to cry.

'But,' his grandpa went on, 'we just voted on a course of action. If I may have the lamp . . . ?'

So the lamp was snuffed out, and lit again with the words 'Irving Willig', and to Dylan's enormous relief the quiet attention was transferred to Grandpa. The whole group listened, but he was mostly speaking to Dylan.

'We've just agreed a silver tithe among those present,' he began, 'to buy you passage on a landman ship.' Merlin tutted audibly at this. Tithes, a collection of silver to sell to landmen, were a rare measure, used only when landman currency suddenly became a necessity. They were never popular. But Grandpa Willig ignored Merlin; he was looking at Dylan with painful hope. 'We thought we might find something that would get you close enough to smokers for you to find your way, and harvest sea-silver. I've been looking at sea maps. We were thinking a New York passage, which would pass near the most northerly smokers on the Ridge . . . You know them?'

'Yes!' said Dylan. He knew the plains of the northern Atlantic well, and he knew where to find the northern-most smokers: there was a vast mountain chain stretching across the whole Atlantic floor, the Ridge, and a valley running through its heart, where from one familiar slab of rock the smokers sprouted like trees.

'And can you harvest,' said Grandpa, 'in your . . . state?'

'Yes,' said Dylan. 'As long as I have a kobold net.'

'Right. Good. Well – this seems like a possibility, then . . .' said Grandpa.

'Definitely,' said Dylan, trying to look assured. The idea of more delay panicked him a little, but this was the only way to get more silver, and there was no way now that he could reach the Sargasso without curing himself first. And the seabed didn't frighten him, even if it should, now that he was prey-sized. But the thought of being sent alone on to a strange landman ship, where his freshwater relatives couldn't follow, made him want to cling to his grandpa like a little boy.

'But –' began Uncle Firth – then remembered etiquette, raised a hand to speak, and stood when Grandpa Willig nodded to him. 'Dylan can't go in the sea. The hag . . .'

'Yes. The folk did say,' said Grandpa Willig. 'I asked if they could kill the thing, but they seem to think that's almost impossible ... We thought perhaps the ship would give sufficient head start? But of course, if there is any danger it can move that fast, we must reconsider ...' And he looked at Dylan questioningly.

'I'm sure it can't,' said Dylan. In truth, he had no idea. But it was hard to believe the tiny hag could follow him at such speeds out into open ocean. And anyway, it was the only plan they had. Uncle Firth looked at him uncertainly, but squatted down again as Grandpa Willig resumed.

'The merfolk,' he said, 'have offered to meet you by the smokers – at the lip of the valley in the Ridge, they said? – with weapons. They have sent their light signals out to those of their number who are furthest out to sea, who will have set out already. I gather they refuse to go near the smokers themselves, but they would be on hand above to assist you if there were a – a chase . . .' Here Grandpa Willig caught Uncle Firth's stony expression, and faltered.

'If the folk think Dylan needs a guard,' said Uncle Firth, not bothering to raise his hand, 'then this isn't safe.'

'The plan's nonsense from start to finish,' said long-faced Merlin, unfolding himself forwards. 'If all the other wyrms' – he almost whispered this word, thick with distaste – 'couldn't fight this thing, why are we sending the smallest one off to die with the others?'

Dislike rose up strongly in Dylan. 'I don't have to fight it,' he said. 'I just have to release my family. It traps them with pieces of current, like a spider web. If I get them out while it's away or asleep, there doesn't have to be a fight.'

Uncle Firth picked up again as though Merlin hadn't

spoken. 'Dylan, if that hag finds you in the sea, you'll drown . . .'

'Landman ships are fast. I'll be fine.'

Uncle Firth seemed to weigh this a moment. Then he looked at Grandpa Willig. 'We'll need enough silver for my passage too – a return ticket.' And in reply to Dylan's silent surprise, he said, 'Don't be daft, you're not going alone. I can take a barrel of fresh water. I'll be fine.'

The great salted expanse of the sea was the ultimate horror to amphibious silvermen. Dylan felt he should tell his uncle that he didn't have to do it, but the words wouldn't come out. He was too grateful. He didn't want to go alone.

In the pause, Grandpa Willig took the reins again. 'We thought you might say that, Firth – we should have enough,' he said. 'Eyre will be back tonight, and we can pawn the silver in the morning. If there's a suitable ship, and you're willing, Dylan, then this is our offer to you.'

A dozen grave faces turned to Dylan, and waited. Even the faces that were annoyed seemed interested, curious to see what sort of person this child of the Weard would prove to be. For a moment even Dylan wondered – he had never really been challenged, before. Dangerous jobs were for his parents, and now his sisters. They had always kept him safe.

They had kept him inside their own tiny world, where none of their lives were ever subject to a vote, and the sea was never a dirty word spat between pursed lips, and Dylan was never an object of curiosity. And they might not come home.

'Thank you,' said Dylan. 'Yes. Of course I'll go.'

*

Eyre, a beaming young woman, returned with excited news of a ship called the SS *Rose Marie*: a tramp steamer, whatever that was, with wool cargo bound for the city called New York. The main advantage of this ship, she explained, was that the landman who brokered the deal seemed willing to accept currency for passage on board without worrying about something called a passport, as long as they increased the price a little. But they would have to be ready to board first thing the next day.

So the chittering dispersed, and Grandpa Willig found bed rolls for Uncle Firth and Dylan, while Uncle Firth went out for his first proper dive since they had left the loch. When he came back in, he and Dylan laid out the bed rolls one after the other down the long galley, and lay facing inwards, so that their heads met in the middle. When Meriel and Tor and Dylan had all been small enough to visit, they would lie like this, but with the twins squeezed next to each other. Dylan had a memory, one of those momentary fragments, of the fan of their red hair glinting in the light of a passing boat. Now there was just Uncle Firth, already asleep and snoring his light, apologetic snore – as though, in his sleep, he was sorry to disturb you.

Dylan couldn't drift. His mind was full, and the hagflesh had begun a new dull, throbbing ache. After an hour of staring at the ceiling, feeling the gentle lull of the boat, he propped himself up on one elbow and checked the blood vials in their tin: no change. Then, very quietly, he eased himself up and padded across the galley, out on to the deck. He wanted to look at the water. It always helped, when he was away from home, to be near water.

It did help, but the faded stars and distant night-noises of the city were strange. He wondered what landman ships were like. At least he would be surrounded by the sea. The water here lay still and inert.

Then, suddenly, the surface of the water was torn in two. There was a noise like metal on metal, and the flesh on Dylan's wrist squeezed so tightly that it brought him to his knees.

The hag was much, much larger now, a long rope of muscle. It flung itself at the side of the boat with a horrible heavy thud. It came nowhere near the deck, and smacked hopelessly back into the water; but it tried again, and again, and again, more bruised and bloodied each time it burst from the dock. Dylan knelt on the deck, frozen, watching in horror. Every time the thing hit the boat or the water, the pieces of hagflesh at his wrist and rib writhed in pain, pulling at his own flesh horribly. But still the hag tried again, and again, with relentless determination.

It must have thrown itself against the wood at least a dozen times. Its last efforts barely cleared the water – it grew dazed and sluggish. At last, with a frustrated swirl of surface-water, it subsided.

The pain at Dylan's wrist began to ebb.

A creak from behind made him jump – but it was the door, and Uncle Firth's head poking out.

'What was that?' he said blearily. He was still half asleep.

Thoughts flitted fast across Dylan's mind – of his uncle's anxious panic after the hag attack; of his uncertain frown when they had discussed the dangers of the hag at the chittering; of the absolute necessity of boarding the next ship to take him out across the Atlantic, whatever the dangers, and whatever over-protective uncles might want to insist.

'Wind,' he lied lamely. Luckily, Uncle Firth was not awake enough to consider this very thoroughly. He nodded, then looked at the night around him, as though observing a gently baffling dream.

'Not enough stars here,' he said.

'True.'

'You're all right?'

'Fine. Just needed some air.'

'Mm.' Uncle Firth looked, for a moment, as though he might break out of his half-sleeping state, and find something more to say. But then he nodded again, and shut the door.

Dylan looked back at the water, his heart still pounding. The pain at his wrist had subsided. The water was still.

9

Dylan, Uncle Firth and Grandpa Willig travelled by bus to the docks. They spent the journey mostly in silence, unable to use the words nál or hag or wyrm or Weard while sleepy landmen crowded around them. Dylan sat with his face to the window; sometimes the bus took a turn and the Thames came into sight, slow and broad and brackish. Was the hag in there, following?

He had resolved not to tell Uncle Firth about its appearance at the docks until the ship was underway. But his mind was crowded with it – with the smacking against the boat, and the desperate rasping, and above all the way the thing had grown. He knew nothing of how a hag behaved after it had been fed. Would it keep growing? What else might it become capable of, now it had his spirit to feed on?

The bus journey felt too short: he was not ready when they arrived at the docks, and Grandpa Willig – with great care – rang the bell. They bumped and apologised their way off the bus with all their luggage, Uncle Firth carefully shuffling a full barrel of water and trying not to crush anybody's feet, and they stepped out on to the pavement. The bus pulled away and left them there.

The Thames was hidden from view here, but the air smelled of salt. It made both the silvermen wrinkle up their noses, but something in Dylan stirred a little, and he had a comforting memory of strength, and of weaving confidently through great currents and valleys. For a moment he could almost sense the tide. This was where he belonged.

'Right then,' said Uncle Firth. 'Let's find this ship.'

The docks were crowded and busy and somehow shapeless: flat mud met flat yawning river, and people milled about in ways that gave the place no overall direction. Boxes and crates swung through the air on cranes, and men heaved and shouted, and alongside it all the Thames shrugged its way out to the sea. Along its banks, ships waited.

The trick was to find the right one, in all the shapelessness. They were weighed down by new luggage in addition to their own cases, pressed on them by Grandpa Willig – tools for navigation, and a kobold skin for the silver harvest, and spare jumpers and fly silks, and all the dried and pickled food he could find and force on them. But the real trouble was Uncle Firth's barrel of water, which had to be rolled through the crowds without knocking over anyone or crushing anything. They had been colourfully sworn at by several people by the time Dylan spotted their ship at last.

'That one!' he said, pointing to a ship with SS *Rose Marie* emblazoned on the hull. Uncle Firth threw himself bodily over the barrel to bring it to a halt, and they all stood, and craned up at the ship. It was grey all over, except where rust and lead had speckled it red, and the top deck was a confusion of funnels and mast and cranes. It could not have been less like a silverman houseboat.

Beside Dylan, Uncle Firth stared up for a few seconds at the alien ship in grim silence. Then he nodded, as though silently deciding something. 'Well,' he said, dumping his bags on top of the barrel, 'here we are. I'll find out who we need to speak to.'

This was easier said than done. There was a confusion of people, and towers of crates, and no obvious way of telling who was involved with what. Uncle Firth approached the nearest person – a girl Dylan's age, who seemed unlikely to be the person they needed, but who pointed confidently across the mud at a knot of men – then he set off where she pointed.

Grandpa Willig had also put his bags down with a grunt, and he looked at Dylan now with his fingertips pressed together, mouth open to speak. But he seemed a little lost for words. This was unsettling: Grandpa Willig was never lost for words.

'Well, Dylan,' he said at last, 'you've understood the route? And you know how to use the sextant to check coordinates – a star sight – yes? Yes, of course.' He lapsed back into silence, then tried again. 'Dylan. I know the pressures are very great, but I hope you don't feel – that is, if this isn't safe, I wouldn't want you to – your parents wouldn't want –'

Dylan wished he would stop. 'It's all right,' he said. 'Really. I'm acting Weard now – it's my responsibility.'

This was not the kind of reassurance Grandpa had wanted, and he pushed his fingertips tighter. 'I'm quite sure this hag can't have kept pace with you all the way down here,' he said, speaking a little too fast, and too loudly. 'And these landman ships are very fast – it can't follow, surely. Getting the silver will be quite safe. And then – well, this nál is routine, isn't it? The others were taken by surprise. But you won't be. And you're the strongest, your mam says, in your other form. And perhaps some of the others of your kind are still nearby, they could help . . .'

Dylan didn't know what he could say that would stop the babble, so he just repeated, 'It's all right, Grandpa.'

'But if it *is* dangerous, Dylan . . . I mean, of course it is, but if it's *too* dangerous . . .' His fingers twisted a moment. 'I would never have forgiven myself if we didn't try to help you rescue my Dougie, and your mam and the girls. But I will never forgive myself if you don't come back.'

'There'll be nothing to forgive yourself for,' said Dylan. 'This is my job. You didn't invent the Weard.'

'Yes . . . yes.' Then Grandpa Willig looked at the sky, and added, 'My little boy . . .'

Dylan wasn't sure if he was the little boy in question, or if his dad was. He thought it was probably Dad. Part of Grandpa still saw Dad as a boy, just as Dad would never quite stop seeing Dylan as *his* little boy, and telling him to be good and stay safe . . .

Dylan's eyes were suddenly filling with tears, and he looked away, blinking hard. He noticed that the girl who had directed Uncle Firth was now watching them with interest. His cheeks burned; he looked back at Grandpa Willig, for want of a better option.

'You don't think this hag could follow you to sea – do you?' pleaded Grandpa Willig.

But at that moment Uncle Firth reappeared, beckoning, and Dylan was relieved of the need to answer.

'I'd better go,' he said. 'Bye, Grandpa.'

'Yes, 'said Grandpa, 'right you are. Well, then. Good fortune, child of the Weard.' And he stepped forward, and squeezed Dylan tightly. Then he helped the two of them to load themselves up with all the bags, and they tramped away from him across the mud, Uncle Firth rolling the barrel before them.

Dylan half expected to be called back. But when he looked back his grandpa was still standing there, hands clasped, watching him go.

A sullen man led Dylan and Uncle Firth up the gangplank, waiting impatiently while Uncle Firth struggled with the barrel. The ship was a continuation of the chaos on the docks. Great hatches were open in the deck to reveal cargo holds below, and cranes were lowering boxes and crates inside.

The man pointed to the fore of the ship. Past the cranes, Dylan could see the steel wall at the end of the deck, with a steel door set into it; on either side of the door, ladders led up to the arrowhead of raised deck above.

'Passenger rooms are below decks at the fo'c'sle,' said the man. Satisfied with this explanation, he left to join the shouting and waving around the cranes and cargo, leaving the two passengers to weave their own cargo through the bustle to the door.

The door was heavy, and led to a cramped corridor with three more doors on either side. Some of them were numbered.

'Did anyone tell you which was ours?' Dylan asked.

'Nope,' said Uncle Firth. 'No one's told me anything much.' He started pushing doors. The first door, marked 'Infirmary', was locked. One of the numbered doors was also locked, but the other two revealed two identical cabins. The blank doors led to a toilet and a bath.

'Oh!' said Dylan, when he saw the bath. 'Proper plumbing! We have these in houses, landmen wash in them . . .' Uncle Firth looked underwhelmed, so he explained, 'It might mean fresh water.' And he went through the door his uncle held open, into the little white-box room with a small high porthole. He turned on the tap, and put a hand experimentally into the flow.

His skin fizzled faintly. 'Ah,' he said. 'Sorry, false alarm. Salt water.'

Uncle Firth just nodded, with the air of someone who has been pushing a barrel all morning, and no longer cares about anything in the world apart from sitting down. 'Which cabin d'you want?' he said. 'Since no one's told us . . .'

They inspected them, but there was very little to choose between them. They felt like little tin cans. In each there were four hard bunks, clamped two on each side to the longer walls; at the far end, opposite the door, there was a chest of drawers topped by a porthole. Dylan chose the one that felt marginally friendlier, mostly because it was currently getting the most light, and he put his case on a lower bunk. Uncle

Firth dropped his own case on the other, then went back out and painstakingly shuffled the barrel; there was no room to roll it.

Dylan took the tin of blood vials from his coat pocket, and looked inside. The blood was still churning quietly. Overhead, footsteps crossed the raised deck, and men shouted indistinctly, and far above them all a gull gave a ragged cry.

Uncle Firth finally sat, with a little huff of exhaustion, on the bed opposite Dylan.

'Uncle Firth,' said Dylan. 'Is this – is it going to work?'

He surprised himself with the question – a useless question, and a shamefully young one. Of course they couldn't know. That was not how the Weard thought: you simply took the best course of action available. But panic had suddenly surged in Dylan, like the crest of a wave that has travelled quietly across the ocean for a long time, and it had risen up out of him in the form of a question before he could stop it.

Uncle Firth had only got as far as shifting forward on his bunk, gathering a reply, when there was a sharp knock on the door. They both jerked their heads, surprised.

There was a pause, then footsteps, then the dull sound of knocking further along. Someone was trying each door in turn.

'Should we – answer it?' Dylan whispered, his mind still unbalanced by the cresting panic.

'Yes,' said Uncle Firth, standing wearily. 'It'd look strange to hide away.' He stood, opened the door, and looked out into the corridor. 'Hello! Are you looking for us?'

The man who came to the door wore the sort of jacket and cap that suggested importance, and a look in his eyes that

Dylan had seen before, on people who did jobs for money: neither friendly nor unfriendly, but disconcertingly – absent. Below the eyes he was mostly dark curly beard.

'Good afternoon,' he said. 'I am Captain Groves.'

'Hello!' said Uncle Firth. 'Firth Pade.'

'Dylan,' said Dylan.

Captain Groves nodded with polite indifference. 'I have come to welcome you aboard the SS *Rose Marie*.'

'Delighted to be here,' said Uncle Firth.

This did not require a nod, so the captain continued without pause. 'I must inform you of a few particulars,' he said. 'You will find a lavatory and bath on this deck. Meals are served in the mess, which you will find at the aft of the ship. Breakfast at eight bells, luncheon at two bells, dinner at five bells. Passengers are not permitted in the cargo holds or engine rooms. Do you have any questions for me?'

Dylan and Firth exchanged a brief glance. But it seemed safest to appear very familiar with everything and not ask any stupid questions, so Dylan shook his head.

'Very good. One other matter' – Captain Groves' tone shifted very subtly from indifferent-polite, to indifferent-stern. 'I am informed that you brought a barrel on board.' They all looked at the barrel, and the captain went on, 'May I enquire as to the contents?'

For a half-second, Dylan wondered whether they ought to lie, although he couldn't exactly see why or how. But Uncle Firth spoke first, and said truthfully, 'Fresh water.'

The polite-sternness stiffened very slightly. 'We have sufficient drinking water on board,' said Captain Groves.

'It's for bathing,' said Dylan quickly. 'My uncle has a – skin condition. Easily irritated.'

Uncle Firth nodded at this, a little too enthusiastically, as though having a skin condition struck him as a really excellent idea. There was a moment's strained silence.

'I am sure you will appreciate,' said Captain Groves, 'that I will need to confirm this. We are obliged to ensure our vessel isn't used for the trading of any contraband substances.'

'Of course,' said Uncle Firth. 'Please, be my guest.' And he stepped back to let Captain Groves into the cabin, and opened up the barrel for inspection.

It *was* full of water, of course; but still Dylan found his heart was beating somewhere in his stomach, and it stayed there the whole time the captain was peering and touching and sniffing and tasting and rummaging around – as though somehow, he might straighten up and say, indifferently, 'I see – it appears that you are a monster and must be hunted with harpoons. I am sure you understand.' But of course, he didn't. When he had finished he just frowned slightly, puzzled – then seemed to decide he had done his duty, and returned to indifference.

'Very good,' he said. 'Please stay aboard the vessel from now on. We expect to depart shortly.' And with this, he touched his cap, ducked back out of the door, and was gone.

They listened as his footsteps rang down the corridor, and the outside door slammed shut. Uncle Firth let out a sort of deflating *phew* sound, as though he had been holding his breath. 'Well, seems like we passed,' he said. 'I might refresh my skin' – he began pulling off his jumper – 'I know I can't be dry yet, but the smell of all that salt . . .'

'I love that smell,' said Dylan. 'I think I'll go up on deck and get some more of it. I need the air.'

'Monster,' said Firth, muffled by wool.

'Frog,' retorted Dylan, automatically, as his uncle emerged from the jumper looking rumpled and tired.

'Well, be careful,' said Uncle Firth. 'And before we were interrupted, I was going to say' – he looked as serious as he could, with his hair now sticking up in every direction at once – 'I think you are doing the best thing you *can* do, and that you are showing a great deal of wisdom and courage.'

Dylan didn't argue. 'Thanks.'

'And I do think it will very possibly work.'

Dylan thought about mentioning the hag in the water. He imagined Uncle Firth's horrified face, and he couldn't quite find the words. 'Thanks,' he said again.

'You're all right?'

'I'm all right.'

'Good. Now off you go and breathe your foul salty air.'

'Enjoy your puddle.' Dylan stood; then he paused at the door, and added, 'Thanks for coming with me.'

But Uncle Firth had plunged his head into the barrel, and didn't hear him.

10

The ship was preparing for departure. The hatches had been closed, and the cranes folded away into their resting state. A couple of dozen men were gathered on the deck, listening as Captain Groves gave a lecture that was lost to Dylan under the noise of the dock.

This gave him a moment to tour the ship in relative isolation. He made the most of it. He found he could follow the deck as far as the middle of the ship, picking his way round mast and cranes and ventilators and miscellaneous ropes and chains. At midships he was obliged to climb a sort of ladder-stairway and cross along a raised deck, before climbing back down again to continue. The whole ship was shaped like a W, with raised sections at the fore and aft, and the highest section of all in the middle – topped by a funnel for the steam and, to Dylan's dismay, some sort of watch room overlooking the decks. He hadn't yet given much thought to anything that happened above the waves beyond getting passage on the ship. Slipping off it and back on again without attracting attention, he now realised, was going to be a problem.

This was, at least, the kind of problem that could in theory be solved. It soothed him to concentrate on it. He strolled the deck with his best casual air, assessing. At the aft of the ship they stored, for some reason, a small rowing boat; if he stepped behind that and slipped below the bottom rail, he thought the boat might keep him from the view of the watch room, but he wasn't certain. And he would still need this part of the deck to be empty of people . . .

He leaned against the rail, and looked out. He could almost have touched the Thames, if he had squatted down and put a hand below the lowest bar. It was silty and slow, but the salt smelled wonderful, scraping his lungs clean with every breath.

He looked over his shoulder, then checked the tin of vials again. No change. He tucked them safely in his inside pocket, and turned back to the Thames.

There was a flash of movement in the turgid water.

His heart pounded, and he stumbled backwards. But the hag didn't appear. A moment later, the movement came again, and this time he saw the cause: a very human, grey pair of eyes surfaced, gazing up at him under sandy hair. Dylan squatted down, and pressed his face against the railings.

'Caspian?'

The head emerged a little more. Not Caspian – this man was older, with a beard. But merfolk. Dylan glanced around instinctively. The man was hidden from the bank by the hull of the boat, but this was still absurdly risky.

'Child of the Weard,' said the man – just loudly enough to

be heard. Dylan pressed his face harder against the cool metal of the railing bars, as though this would get him closer.

'Do you have news? Is something wrong?' His mind raced. Mam, Dad, Meriel, Tor. Found? In what state?

The man's face was unreadable, bobbing gently on the brown water. 'I have come to advise you,' he said. 'The nál grows more powerful, and the seas bend south towards it. The ship may travel faster than you expect.'

'Oh! Do you know how long it'll take to the smokers?'

'It is not yet clear.'

'Right. Right. Thank you.' Dylan wished the man *had* been Caspian. This man was much more typical of merfolk, unfriendly and unreadable. The hagflesh was throbbing again; he ignored it. 'There's no news of my family?'

'No,' said the man. He was no longer looking at Dylan, scanning the deck instead for any onlookers. 'I must leave before I am seen. Fortune, child of the Weard.'

'I –'

But silently, without causing the slightest ripple on the surface, the man was gone.

Dylan didn't want him to be gone. There must be more to say, more news of the world at sea. He was so absorbed in watching the water, scanning the ripples for any sign of the man below, that it was a shock when someone spoke behind him on the deck.

'Who were you talking to?'

He looked around. It was a girl he recognised, but it took a moment to place her. She was the girl from the docks, the one who had given Uncle Firth directions – the one who had been staring at him when he cried.

He straightened up quickly, trying to look casual. This was not helped by a painful twinge of the flesh at his ribs as he stood. She was looking at him with hungry curiosity, and it was disconcerting – he found his cheeks burning again, even though he wasn't crying this time.

'No one,' he said.

'You were talking to someone in the sea,' she insisted. Something about her told Dylan immediately that she wasn't going to be easy to lie to.

She stared at him openly, so he stared back. Her face was round and pale like a full moon, somehow at odds with her tall strong frame. Dark curls escaped an ineffectual plait. She made him think of the way landmen drew mermaids and sea goddesses.

Dylan looked away first. 'I wasn't,' he said, scrabbling for a story. 'I was talking to myself. I get homesick. I'm nervous about leaving. I was just sort of – encouraging myself.'

She stared at him for a few seconds longer.

'I'm Dylan,' said Dylan, to fill the silence.

'Rose,' said the girl.

'Ah. Like the ship,' said Dylan. Which wasn't, he felt, the best thing he had ever said. But he was reeling from the man's sudden appearance and disappearance, and the news he had brought; and the hagflesh was really hurting now; and something about this girl's stare made his face flush and his mind go a bit stupid. So all he could think of by way of follow up was, 'The ship's called the *Rose Marie*. So – you're both Rose.'

The girl didn't comment. 'You're in the passenger rooms?'

'Yes – cabin two.'

'You're next to me then. Is that man with you your dad?'

'My uncle.'

Rose considered this. 'Where're your parents?'

Dylan had a feeling that this was a lot of questions, even for a landman. But it didn't feel rude, somehow; it just felt – interested. Powerfully interested. The sort of interest that most people reserve for themselves, turned outwards.

Rude or not, this was an uncomfortable line of questioning. 'They're – I'm on my way to join them.'

'They're in New York?'

He had forgotten what the place was called, and nodded gratefully. 'Yes. New York. We're moving there.'

'Why?'

'New job,' said Dylan. It was an effort to lie at the speed of her questions.

'You happy about it?'

'Yes. It's really good. Yeah.'

She considered him a moment, then came to lean against the rails beside him. 'You're a terrible liar,' she said. 'I'm not sure if I believe you about the job. I definitely don't believe that you're happy – you look like you're about to be sick. And you *were* talking to someone in the sea.'

Dylan couldn't think of anything at all to say to this, and the flesh at his wrist now pulled so sharply that he had to set his teeth against it to avoid gasping. He glanced over his shoulder at the water – nothing there – and the girl followed his gaze, then looked at him with eyebrows raised.

'I'm not lying,' was all Dylan could think of. The pain was making his eyes water.

Maybe Rose noticed; she sounded a little softer when she replied. 'You are. But never mind. I've got a whole voyage to get it out of you. Do you want to talk about why you're so unhappy instead?' And when Dylan didn't reply, she added, 'And don't say you're all right, because if you lie to me again, I'm pitching you overboard.'

'It's nothing,' said Dylan. 'What about you? Why are you going to New York?'

'Don't change the subject,' she said.

'No really, I want—'

'I'll tell you all about me, when you give me a single straight answer. Tell me what's wrong. You'll feel better.'

'I'm homesick,' said Dylan. 'And I miss my family.' It was all he could think of. It was also not technically a lie.

Maybe she could smell the truth in it, because although she looked at him for a long moment, she didn't object. Instead she leaned in a little closer – and his heart was beating strangely; he could feel the pulse against the pressing flesh on his wrist, heavy and too fast – and said, 'I prescribe a friend, then.' And she smiled at Dylan, and it seemed to him that she was very soft and very close. There was a little silence, so he opened his mouth to reply, and sincerely hoped that whatever he was about to say wasn't going to be stupid.

He never found out; happily, he was rescued by the appearance of Uncle Firth. Less happily, Uncle Firth was sopping wet. He had forgotten to put on shoes, his shirt clung to his chest, and his hair had become a sort of wilted hedgehog, which was dripping with a merry patter on the deck.

Rose stared at him – which at least gave Dylan a brief reprieve.

'Hello,' said Uncle Firth, smiling distractedly at Rose. 'Dylan – could I have a quick word? Back at the cabin?'

'*Yes*,' said Dylan gratefully. He stepped quickly away from the rails. 'See you,' he said to Rose – trying his best to sound like somebody normal, who just talks to the sea in a normal sort of way, and wasn't currently being crushed by malevolent flesh.

She nodded, and said, 'See you.' Dylan wished Uncle Firth had thought to take some basic precautions to look ordinary – he had a feeling he was going to have a lot more lies to invent the next time he saw Rose. At midships he glanced back. Captain Groves was at the railings now, talking to her; but even as she replied to the captain, she was watching him and Uncle Firth as they walked away.

Dylan followed his uncle back along the ship. He kept scanning the water, but he saw nothing, and the pain had begun to ease, although he still felt sore. It became easier to think clearly. If the ship was going to move faster, he'd better take a star sight tonight . . . He opened his mouth to tell Uncle Firth about it, saw his uncle's expression, and changed his mind.

'What's happening?' he said.

'You'll see,' said Uncle Firth.

'Is it bad?'

Uncle Firth shrugged a little helplessly at that.

'There's news? Something about the others?'

'No no, nothing like that.' And Dylan thought for a moment that Uncle Firth might say more – but then the floor under their feet began to thrum, and they both started in surprise. The walls vibrated too. The whole *world* vibrated.

'Ship's engines,' said Dylan. 'We're underway.'

'Right,' said Uncle Firth. 'Right.' Then, 'Bother – I was hoping we could get rid of it. Maybe we still can . . .'

He started walking to their cabin, and Dylan hurried after him. 'Get rid of what? Uncle Firth? Get rid of what?'

By way of reply, Uncle Firth opened the cabin door, and jerked his head. Dylan stepped inside.

For a brief moment, a horse was crammed awkwardly between the bunks. Then it shimmered, and a naked man stood in its place, hair tangled and wild, palms wide as though in supplication.

'Dylan,' said the kelpie, pronouncing carefully. 'Dylan Pade.'

11

Dylan stared at the kelpie. The kelpie stared at Dylan. Uncle Firth dripped and stomped across the cabin, to where the bags lay in half-opened confusion.

'I was trying to find the defensive silver,' he said, 'but I don't suppose it will help. Do you know what *will* help?'

'You're not really meant to get rid of them,' said Dylan.

'I don't give a minnow's fart about the etiquette, I am not living with a salting *kelpie* on a landman ship in the middle of the *sea*.' Uncle Firth's voice rose in both volume and pitch as he said this, and his rummaging through the bags became more energetic and much less effective. On 'sea' he knocked a half-open case off the bunk in his haste, spilled the contents everywhere, and swore loudly.

The kelpie turned its huge sombre eyes to him. They were disconcerting eyes, at once deeply alive and entirely blank. It felt as though you were looking at the eye of a hurricane, and everything really important was swirling just out of sight.

Dylan knelt down to help pick things up. Gently, he tried to explain. 'It's not just the etiquette thing. If they really try to offer you help, you're meant to take it. They're kind of wise about some things.'

Uncle Firth did not reply, in the loudest way possible. Dylan tried again. 'It was trying to help back in the cottage, remember? We didn't realise, so we didn't listen. But it didn't want the others to leave.'

'Right,' said Uncle Firth, flinging things back into the case. 'And has it come to collect the price for that little titbit of wisdom?'

'What do you mean?'

'Kelpies take blood sacrifice, Dylan, they aren't just salting saints wandering around helping people for free.'

Dylan looked at the kelpie, which was watching their movements with grave interest. The River Lore did say that about kelpies – if you wanted a ride. Not just for advice. But still.

'*Do* you want blood?' said Dylan.

The kelpie shook its head.

'Are you here to help?'

A nod.

'Why?'

The kelpie considered this, then said carefully, 'Weard.' It put one fist to its chest.

Dylan's gut clenched. The kelpies did not help the Weard trivially, but some old stories did speak of them assisting when there was a particularly significant threat. If the kelpies thought it was time to intervene, that was not reassuring.

'Why won't it talk properly?' snarled Uncle Firth.

'We're not sure,' said Dylan. 'It seems to cost them something to learn to make human words. It can do names, and titles, and weather.' And the kelpie smiled a little shyly at this and nodded, as though Dylan had paid it a compliment.

Uncle Firth crossed his arms mulishly, and stared past the creature, at the far wall. 'I don't see why. Selkies can talk. You can talk.' And when Dylan stared at him in surprise, he quickly added, 'Sorry. I know that's not the same. I just – sorry, Dylan.'

Silverman taxonomy lumped all the shapeshifters together – as though a kelpie and a wyrm should have anymore in common than horses and people. But Uncle Firth knew better. And it was insulting to be compared to a selkie, which prattled convincingly like a human but thought like a water-creature; never mind a kelpie, whose human shape was so obviously a trick of flesh. There was a short, awkward silence.

The kelpie seemed to think its right to join them was now settled, and it had seated itself cross legged on the floor, gazing placidly at the wall. But Uncle Firth was not finished.

'You know they drown landmen sometimes?' he said. 'Just for fun?'

Dylan shrugged helplessly. 'Yes. I know. But – we could really use its help.'

Uncle Firth shut his eyes, and for a few seconds seemed to be deciding whether to speak.

'Do you know,' he said at last, 'why your mam won't have them around?'

'No . . .'

'She said she didn't want to tell you when you were small,'

said Uncle Firth, 'with kelpies so common round the cottage. Said it would give you all nightmares. I didn't know if she'd told you since. I always thought she should. She doesn't like to remember – but we *should* remember.'

Dylan just waited. There was something fragile in the way Uncle Firth spoke, which told him the slightest interruption might knock this explanation off course, and send his uncle back to hunting for protective silver and yelling unhelpfully.

'They killed your great-uncle, Dylan,' he said. 'It was a blood sacrifice, for helping some silvermen.'

Dylan had known that Uncle Abe had died when Mam and Auntie Isla had been fleeing for Scotland; he had not known how. He opened his mouth to ask more, but the kelpie was looking at Uncle Firth with interest too – and now, as though remarking on the weather, it commented, 'Aberforth Pade.'

Uncle Firth was on his feet in a moment. 'Don't you ever say that name again,' he spat. 'Kelpie scum.'

The kelpie turned its eyes to Dylan in confused appeal, and explained, 'Aberforth Pade.'

Uncle Firth dived. With an indignant shudder, the kelpie changed into a horse, and Dylan had to quickly hold on to his uncle to stop him attempting to engage a large horse in fisticuffs. 'Uncle Firth – stop, you can't . . . It's a *wind spirit*. Hitting it won't help.'

'Uncle Abe was the best man I have ever known,' said Uncle Firth, still shouting, as though he could punch at the kelpie just with the force of his lungs. 'They killed him in cold blood. They *demanded* his life. That's what kelpies do, Dylan, they're heartless murderers, and I will *not* share a cabin with that thing. I won't do it. I want it off this ship.'

Dylan was poised to hold Uncle Firth back again. But quite suddenly he took a great sobbing breath in and subsided on to the bed, head in hands, his anger spent. Dylan could only hover, not knowing what you were supposed to say to an uncle who had suddenly become a small hurt boy right in front of your eyes. He put an awkward hand on one shaking shoulder: no response.

Quietly, a little sheepishly, the kelpie shimmered into a man. It put its fist to its chest again, and bowed its head a moment.

Dylan pulled his gaze from Uncle Firth, and looked at the kelpie's fist, then its hurricane eyes. Kelpies *were* killers, sometimes. But he couldn't afford to turn away a powerful spirit right now – whatever Uncle Firth might feel.

'You won't ask for blood, if you help?' he said quietly. 'This is freely given?'

The kelpie nodded.

'Things are that bad, then?'

It nodded again, emphatically.

'Is it true you can see the future?'

This time it wobble-nodded, and seemed to search its vocabulary. It settled on, 'Fog.'

'So, partially? A bit fuzzy?'

The kelpie sighed, as though saddened by the great inadequacy of this description, and repeated the wobble-nod.

'All right,' said Dylan. 'So – how are you planning to

help?' At this the kelpie became a horse, which looked at him hopefully. 'Oh!' said Dylan, 'You're offering me a ride?'

Uncle Firth emerged from his hands. 'Absolutely not. Being carried by wind is the single most horrifying thing . . .'

'They can only carry as wind over land,' said Dylan. 'I'd have to ride it as a horse over or under water. Right?'

The kelpie nodded again. Nodding looked odd on a horse.

'Still no,' said Uncle Firth.

Dylan had never seen his uncle like this. There was a bleary absence in his eyes, and it did not feel as though he could be reasoned with. Dylan sat down beside him on the bed now, and considered how to say what he must say next as gently as possible. But it couldn't be done, so he just leaned slightly against Uncle Firth, hoping the warmth of human comfort could make up for the helplessness of circumstance.

'I need it,' he said. 'The hag's faster than we thought. It's followed me here.'

This brought Uncle Firth halfway out of his bleariness. He stiffened at Dylan's side. 'How do you know that?'

'It was at the docks last night. It tried to get on the boat.'

'River and moon! Why didn't you say?'

'I didn't want you to stop me going.'

Uncle Firth turned to face Dylan, and his eyes had filled with soft worry in a way so exactly like Mam that Dylan had to look away. 'It's not too late for me to stop you. Dylan, if that thing is fast enough to chase you out here, I am absolutely *not* allowing you to go. You will not be drowning in the Atlantic on my watch. I will lock you in the cabin if I have to.'

'The kelpie would outpace it,' said Dylan. 'Nothing's faster than a wind spirit. If I have the kelpie, I can do this.'

'But—'

'We can assume the nál's got all the other wyrms too, or else someone else would have bound it by now. As far as I can tell it's just me left. If I don't do anything, the Sea loses all its guardians. I have to.'

'Not if it—'

'I won't let them die,' said Dylan. 'I can't go home alone. I won't do it.'

There was a long, long silence at that. In the end, it was the kelpie who spoke first. It spread its hands, and almost timidly, it asked, 'Dylan Pade?'

Dylan looked at his uncle.

'*Fine*,' said Uncle Firth.

And then, as an afterthought, he picked up a boot where it lay among their scattered belongings, and threw it hard at the wall.

NAVIGATION

FROM *THE SEA AND ITS CITIZENS*, DRAFT MANUSCRIPT

Navigation on the seafloor may be managed in the same way as navigation on land: the landmarks of the sea have been extensively mapped by the Weard. What follows is an account of this seabed navigation, but first, it bears mentioning that one landman solution to the problem of sea navigation is highly ingenious. Their measurement system will be useful in comprehending the maps that follow.

The system divides the world into imaginary lines, called latitude when they run north to south, and longitude when they run east to west. By measuring the angle of stars and sun from the horizon, it is possible to determine your place on these lines. This allows you to determine and describe your location anywhere on the earth, including on the formless expanse of the sea.

It is a truly remarkable feat, and typical of the industrious enquiry of landmen. The sea hides every secret it has from them, and still they have refused to be kept to their shores.

12

For most of the afternoon, Uncle Firth slept heavily. Dylan stayed on the deck of the SS *Rose Marie*, watching the land recede until there was only sea and sky. The sky was a pale blue, and the sea was rolling in long low waves. It felt as though the world had been wiped clean.

At intervals, a bell sounded, and men changed places around the ship. When almost all of them went at once to the aft, Dylan guessed it must be dinner. But it was almost dusk, and he needed to be on deck at dusk for his star sight, to find out how far the ship had travelled. Grandpa Willig had packed them some dried food; he would eat that later instead.

He slipped into the cabin, where his uncle snored gently, and he found Grandpa Willig's sextant and chronometer. He emptied a leather travelling bag and packed up the tools, along with the almanac, a notebook and a pencil, then went back outside.

The deck was quiet. He climbed the ladder to the raised deck at the fore, and settled with his back against the railings. Then he consulted the almanac.

It was Dad who had taught him to measure his place on

the globe by the landman scale. It had been almost a game – Tor's idea of course, and Dad had been more than happy to show them, on balmy summer nights. Measuring your latitude was easy, but to calculate your longitude, you needed to be able to see two stars and the horizon – so you couldn't do it in total darkness. It had to be dawn or dusk.

The almanac told Dylan which stars would rise first that night, and where to look for them. He took out Grandpa Willig's sextant – a birthday present from Uncle Firth, for Grandpa's collection of curios. It was a clunking antique, but perfectly functional.

The sun dipped below the horizon, streaking the sky and sea with pink and gold. Dylan scanned the sky for the stars. Rainclouds were gathering to the east, but he was lucky; they didn't obscure the view he needed. He found the first star, put the sextant's telescope to his eye, began adjusting the mirror, and lost himself in measuring the world.

He was good at sums. For a few minutes, his mind was blissfully calm. It was the opposite of the feeling when his sea-spirit was restless: a deep quiet.

When the instruments were back in their case, he double- and triple-checked his numbers, squatting silverman-style over his notebook. The merfolk were right – they were travelling *very* fast. At this speed he would have to go down the next afternoon. Of course, the speed might change; he would have to check again at dawn.

The effect on his mood was immediate. It was much, much better to be doing something. He would have to solve the problem of avoiding the landmen, and prepare the kobold skin, and then he would be underway – and it would be dangerous, but danger was infinitely preferable to waiting, with nothing to occupy him but his thoughts. The hagflesh was pinching again, but even this worried him less now. He had the kelpie. He had a fighting chance.

At the opposite rail, a couple of deckhands had come to watch the last of the sunset, and one called over to Dylan now. 'Strange, isn't it?' he said. 'The speed.'

'Very,' said Dylan.

'Tom's scared.' The man jerked his head at his companion. 'But he's new here. I've seen stranger things at sea. I could tell you a tale or two you wouldn't believe.'

Dylan aimed for a politely-interested 'Oh', that didn't invite the telling of these tales, or give away just how much he certainly *would* believe.

'It's not normal,' was all Tom said.

'No such thing as normal at sea,' said his friend. 'And if we can knock a day or two off this blasted crossing, I'm not complaining. Where'd you learn to take a fix?' he asked Dylan, nodding at the notebook.

'My dad,' said Dylan truthfully.

'He's a seaman?'

'Yes,' said Dylan – half-truthfully.

'Good to see a young lad taking an interest,' said the man. 'Maybe there's a life at sea on the cards for you too, eh? It's not a life for the faint-hearted, mind you – I've seen things – you wouldn't believe half of it, I'm telling you.'

'You're full of hot air, Bill,' said the disgruntled Tom. 'It's freezing. I'm going back below decks.'

His friend – Bill – watched him go a moment, before remarking to Dylan, 'He'll toughen up, in time.' Then he too went down the ladder, whistling to himself.

After that Dylan was alone with the stars and the sea. The sun slipped away entirely, and it was night. The hagflesh twinged especially sharply, and Dylan's thoughts turned inward a moment; he didn't notice the figure in the dark until it stood opposite him.

'There you are,' said Rose. 'You weren't at dinner.' And before he could invent a reason for this, she settled herself down on the deck next to him, and said, 'So. Want to tell me who was in the sea?'

'Nobody,' Dylan tried.

Rose drew her knees to her chest. She was like a little boulder in the dark.

'One night I saw a woman in the sea, about this far out from shore,' she said quietly. 'I wasn't crazy. She was *right there*. She was half-scaly, half-skin.'

Dylan didn't know what to say to this. The Lore forbade talking to landmen of Sea business. But there was no actual advice on what you were meant to do if they insisted on bringing it up. And the pain was making thinking a little difficult.

Rose kept going, undeterred. 'My mother used to see things, before she died. She wasn't well. But this wasn't like the little phantoms and things she used to see. Even she knew they weren't real, really. This was different.'

It felt like she was telling herself this, as much as him. Dylan couldn't get into this conversation. He started to stand, saying, 'I have to go.'

She unfolded quickly, and reached out to grab his wrist. Her hand was right over the hagflesh. Dylan's eyes filled with tears, and he had to bite back a cry.

'I only want to know I'm not crazy,' she said. 'Please. I won't ask you anything else. But I'm not going without that. I'll owe you a favour in return, I swear I'll do whatever you ask. I keep my promises.'

Maybe he just wanted her to let go of his wrist; maybe he felt sorry for her. 'You're not crazy.'

She didn't let go. He could feel her hungry expression, even though he couldn't see it. 'You know what it was?'

'Merfolk.'

'Mer – what?'

'Like what you'd call a mermaid. That hurts – can you –'

She let him go. In the dark he could make out shining eyes, the crescent curve of an elated smile. 'I *knew* you knew something. Who *are* you?'

'No one – I just – know things. I'm just sort of . . . involved with them.'

'With the mermaids? They talk to humans?' And then, when he didn't reply, '*Are* you human?'

This was tricky. Dylan hesitated – a moment too long. He could almost feel Rose's quickening excitement; it seemed to charge the air, and send Dylan's own heart a little faster in reply.

'Then what are you?' she whispered.

Dylan had a muddled feeling he had already said too much, and he wasn't quite sure how it had happened. He hesitated, trying to think straight.

After a moment, she said, 'Sorry. I said I wouldn't ask.

That wasn't fair. Sit back down? Please? I won't ask anything else you can't answer.'

Slightly to his own surprise, Dylan found himself sitting. He drew his knees against his chest, shivering slightly. The sea heaved and sighed, and the world was very still – except inside Dylan, where it wasn't still at all.

'So,' she said, 'I owe you a favour.'

'Oh, no,' said Dylan. 'You don't—'

'I do.' Her face was turned towards him. 'And I'll be very offended if you don't ask for anything.'

River and moon and all the stars. His family were trapped under the Atlantic, and he was being hunted across the sea, and the hagflesh was writhing under his skin, and yet now he had – it was unmistakeable, even though he had never known anything like it before – he had a *crush* on this inquisitive landman girl. There was no room at all for it in his brain, but that didn't stop his pulse from speeding up or his face from flushing or his mind from becoming unhelpfully puddle-like. He hadn't known it could happen to you all at once like that. It was incredibly inconvenient.

'I'll have to try and think of something, then,' he heard himself say.

'Good. I promised we'd be friends, and we can't be friends if it's all out of balance.'

'I suppose not.'

'Maybe I can help with whatever your Big Mission is.'

Dylan breathed in sharply at a particularly stabbing pain in his rib, but he managed, 'What makes you think I've got a Big Mission?'

'You've got all these for fun?' she said, gesturing to his sextant and chronometer and books. 'I bet you know why we're going so fast. If—'

'How did *you* know we're going too fast?'

She waved her hand dismissively. 'The men are all talking about it. Don't change the subject. The mermaid person knew you'd be here. Something's happening.'

'All right,' said Dylan, defeated. He leaned back to feel the cool metal of the rail against the back of his neck, and prepared to explain that nonetheless, there was nothing she could do to help. Then the bells sounded to rearrange the men on their watch, and there were footsteps and shouts – and he remembered that he *did* need help.

He wasn't supposed to talk to landmen about sea business. But he wouldn't need to tell her much. And she'd already guessed a lot. And . . .

'I've got to go into the sea tomorrow,' he found himself saying, before he had exactly made up his mind, 'and get back on board again. I need everyone away from the aft of the ship, so no one sees. Can you think of some sort of – distraction? Whatever counts as an emergency, for – ships . . .' he said. He had nearly said 'for landmen'. But Rose didn't notice the hesitation. She grew more tense next to him, hugging her knees close to her chest in high excitement.

'You can go into the sea?'

'Yes. But you said you wouldn't ask anything . . .'

'I know.' She was staring at him again, and smiling again, and that was very good. 'I won't ask. But I'll help, I'll think of something. When?'

'Mid-afternoon, I think – I'll check our progress at dawn.'
As he spoke, he felt the first spot of rain fall. Two more plopped heavily on the deck.

'Right,' said Rose, ignoring the rain. 'You've asked the perfect person. I'm excellent at causing a scene.'

'I believe it,' said Dylan. 'So where are you – *ahh*' – the hagflesh was suddenly unbearably tight. The bones of his wrist seemed to grind together as it squeezed.

'Are you all right?'

'No,' Dylan admitted. He rocked forward, and knelt for a moment doubled over on the deck, as the rain began to fall around them more heavily. The pain throbbed. He needed sweetflag, or comfrey, or anything that might dull the sensation. He needed Rose to stop looking at him. All the wonderful pulse-racing feeling of a moment ago was gone. He focused, and pushed himself to his feet.

'Sorry,' he said, 'I'm not well. I should go . . .'

Rose stood too. For the first time since he had met her, she looked unsettled. 'I'll see you to your cabin. Do you have something for – whatever's wrong?'

Dylan nodded, which was neither a truth nor a lie but just a reflexive movement, because he wasn't thinking straight anymore. As they crossed the fo'c'sle he hardly noticed Rose's hand at his back, hovering worriedly. He took the ladder mostly one-handed, touching it only limply with his left, and pushed himself through the door below decks, Rose behind him.

'You were cabin two, right?' she said.

Dylan nodded.

'I'm three. Knock if you need anything,' said Rose. 'I hope you're all right.'

'Thanks,' managed Dylan. 'Night. Sorry – I – night.' And he opened the cabin door with his good hand.

Rose opened her mouth to say goodnight. Then she froze, no longer looking at him.

She was looking, instead, over his shoulder. Dylan turned, and saw the naked man-form of the kelpie standing right behind him, its hurricane-eyes huge and dark.

'Ah,' said Dylan. 'Right. That's—'

But he was cut off by the kelpie, which had raised its hand to point at Rose, and begun to bellow. Dylan had never heard a kelpie shout before. It turned out they could be very, very loud.

'Hag!' it cried. It shook its finger at Rose, dark eyes gleaming. 'Hag! Dylan Pade! Hag!'

13

Dylan turned. Rose's full-moon face had fallen open into a little *o* of surprise, and her eyes were big, and suddenly seemed very wild.

Dylan stepped back, shut the door, and turned the key in the lock. He leaned his forehead against the cold metal.

Through the door, Rose said, 'Dylan?' uncertainly.

Behind him, the kelpie insisted, 'Hag.'

'Yes,' murmured Dylan. 'Got it. Thanks.'

Uncle Firth was curled up on his bunk with a book. He propped himself up on one elbow, and said, 'You don't really think . . . ?'

Dylan held up a hand: he was listening. Rose knocked; she tried his name one more time. There was a minute's silence, besides the pattering of rain on the roof and porthole. Then footsteps walked away, and another door opened and shut.

'Hag,' crooned the kelpie.

Uncle Firth glared at it and sat up properly. To Dylan, he said, 'You don't have to listen to that thing. It seems wildly –' he broke off, because the kelpie was singing 'Hag' to itself now, long and low and loud, as though it had forgotten it was currently a horse and was trying to be wind. Uncle Firth's hands were fists. 'Will you salt *off*?'

When shouting had no effect, he threw his book at it. The kelpie looked up at him with sullen hurt, then vanished into wind; after a moment of fluttering book pages, Dylan could no longer tell whether it was still in the cabin. This was probably, overall, for the best. He would have liked to ask it questions, but it didn't seem in the mood to try and be useful, and he could do without it singing 'Hag' for the next hour.

He went to his bunk, and sat with his head in his hands. The pain in his wrists was rapidly subsiding, along with the giddy and inexplicable desire to be near to Rose. How had he been so *stupid*?

'Dylan,' said Uncle Firth, in his most reasonable voice. 'Do you really think it's likely a hag has a human form? Aren't they sort of – big slug things?'

'The human bit could just be a shape,' said Dylan, pressing his palms against his eyelids, 'like for the kelpie. Just something to allow it to survive more than a minute out of water. It doesn't have to mean it's *really* a human.' And why shouldn't it have another shape on land? In the cave, it had been starving – perhaps too weak to transform. It was stronger now. And he knew nothing of a hag at full strength. *This*, said Mam's voice in his mind, *is why you don't feed things that you don't understand.*

'But Rose can talk properly,' objected Uncle Firth.

'Some of the inhuman shifters can do that – like selkies. And spirit-eaters can often borrow things from their prey – forms, and knowledge. It's eating me, and I know how to talk.'

'Well . . .' said Uncle Firth – not convinced.

'It would explain how the hag's been keeping pace,' said Dylan, 'all this way, at this speed. It *could* be capable of that – but if it has a human form, it can just hitch a ride, which sounds a lot easier.' He began ticking off evidence on his fingers. 'We haven't seen anyone travelling with her. She's avoided telling me anything about who she is or where she's going – except her name, which is just the name of the ship, so it's not even a very good lie. The flesh keeps hurting when she's nearby –'

'You *are* also near water,' Uncle Firth interjected, 'which is exactly where we'd expect the hag to be.'

'– and I get this feeling too, like I can't think straight, and like I really want to be near her.' Quickly, he added, 'I know, I know what that sounds like. But I don't think it's that. I think it's some kind of power. Landmen stories are full of alluring shapeshifters.' And when Uncle Firth still looked unconvinced, he said, 'I know you don't like the kelpie. But they *are* future tellers. If it's seen that she's going to transform . . .'

'We don't have to listen to that—'

'We do. Look. I'm sorry they – I'm sorry for what happened. But you *know* they're good at this stuff.'

There was a moment of silence and singing rain; then Uncle Firth sighed, and nodded. 'Yes. All right. Yes. I suppose I do have to be careful not to let prejudice get the better of me. This is important.' He held his hands up, a peace offering. 'I suppose. I do just find this idea hard to get my head around.'

This was understandable. But Uncle Firth had not lived his life around the pulsing forms of the sea, where free spirit infused everything, and almost nothing kept the same shape for long. And he had not felt the way that 'Rose' had blurred Dylan's mind, and drawn him in. Or the sharp tug of flesh.

'I believe the kelpie,' said Dylan.

'Right,' said Uncle Firth, sounding resigned. 'Well – it can't hurt to be careful. I can keep an eye on her, when you go down for silver. Make sure she can't follow.' He didn't say this with conviction, and Dylan wanted to keep arguing, to make his uncle believe him. But if Uncle Firth would act like it was true, that would be something, at least.

'Thanks,' said Dylan. 'I'm going to keep the door locked tonight. I might put those drawers across as a barricade . . .'

Uncle Firth shrugged: indifferent agreement. It was all Dylan was going to get. They sat in silence for a minute then, Dylan absent-mindedly cradling his wrist as the pain subsided into a wounded ache, listening to the rain above their little tin can cabin, and the crash of waves.

It took him a minute to register that nothing in him was stirring at the rain. He was growing used to the quiet. He would miss that, very soon.

'Oh!' he said. 'I forgot to tell you. The merfolk are right. We're going fast – I'll have to go down tomorrow afternoon.'

Uncle Firth's eyes widened. 'So soon? River. All right.'

'I'll check again at dawn. Could you come with me? Keep watch for Rose? I don't think I should risk being alone with her again.'

'Yes, of course.' Quite suddenly, Uncle Firth's serious face half creased into a sly smile. 'I couldn't possibly leave you two alone, now that I know she's using her haggy magic to try and lure you in for a kiss.'

'That is *not*—'

'I know, I know. Sorry. I'm taking it seriously, I promise.' He schooled his face, and said, 'Come on – let's prepare the kobold. And have you eaten? I'm starving. Willig packed food, right . . . ?'

So Dylan joined his uncle on the floor of the cabin, and they unwrapped parcels of food, and spread out the tools for the silver harvest, and began preparing. They didn't talk much, working and munching in companionable silence. It was good to be busy.

A few minutes later, there was a gentle knock on the door. They looked at each other, and Dylan shook his head. They waited in silence, until they heard the footsteps leave once more.

They tried to sleep early, but it felt as though Dylan had barely shut his eyes when the alarm clock was pulling him awake just before dawn. He rolled over blearily. The kelpie was back, sitting between the bunks now, sleeping as a horse.

Dylan shook himself awake and dressed hastily. He put on silverman fly silks, a two-piece set that looked passably close to normal clothes, especially with his jumper on top; he wanted to be ready to dive as soon as he needed to, and since he no longer transformed, he ideally preferred not to return to the ship naked. The porthole glass was swirled with frost, so he bundled the brown blanket from his berth into the bag of tools. Just in case, he laid the kobold skin gently on top.

The skin was fresh and bright red. Kobolds lived underground and belonged properly to Land Lore, but they had one property very useful to the Sea Weard – they gobbled up silver. Even in death, this one would latch over the top of a smoker, and pull out silver at speed.

In the dark beside him, Uncle Firth was dressing. It sounded like he was currently engaged in battle with a particularly troublesome sock. The kelpie whisked itself into wind, but this time Dylan was very aware that it was staying close by his side. He decided not to mention this to Uncle Firth.

When the sock was tamed, they crept out into the corridor. They trod softly past Rose's cabin, breath held. Gently, they eased the heavy outside door shut behind them, and stepped on to the deck.

The rain clouds of the evening before had cleared. It was freezing, and there was a biting wind, and an expectant edge to the dark: dawn was not far off. They hurried up the ladder to the fo'c'sle, metal icy against palms, the ship bucking below them on black waves.

Dylan settled under his blanket while Uncle Firth stood watch, and the kelpie gently fluttered at his side. He was only just in time. There were only a handful of stars remaining, and within minutes, the horizon was visible. He set to work.

He repeated his sums once to make sure he hadn't made a mistake. He would have liked to triple check, but there was no time. Their speed had increased while he slept. He had already overshot the ideal place to dive.

It was time, then. He found that his anxiety stilled suddenly – not calmed, but rather coiled and tensed, ready to spring him into action. He looked at the stirring of air where the kelpie waited. 'We'd better go now,' he said. 'We're late.'

Uncle Firth looked around. 'What? Who are you . . . ? Oh.'

Dylan packed away his things and stood. 'We've sped up. Could you watch Rose's door?'

'You have to go now?'

'We've already gone too far.'

'Yes. Right. River . . . I thought there'd be more time. Well . . .' And Uncle Firth gestured helplessly, as though he had considered a hug, or perhaps a manly shoulder pat, and found them inadequate. 'Be careful,' he said.

'Don't let her out. Swear by the River?' Dylan wished his uncle shared his conviction, but he knew he could at least trust him to keep a promise.

'Yes. I swear.'

'Let's go,' said Dylan.

They went back down the ladder. At the door to the cabins, Uncle Firth hesitated, and did more helpless gesturing. 'It's all right,' said Dylan, reaching out to squeeze his arm. 'I'll be all right.' And then he left his uncle behind, and hurried along the ship to the aft, the gust of the kelpie at his back.

The unexpected timing made things much easier, in one way: everyone but the night watch was asleep, and there was no one at this end of the deck yet. He crouched low behind the rowboat, and at the rail he looked left and right. He saw no one. He pulled a coil of knotted silver thread from his bag, tied it to the rail, and let it uncoil into the water – these were signal knots, and they caused a distinctive bend in the water, to help him find the ship again at a distance. He wasn't at all sure his newly-deafened human skin would be able to feel it, and he didn't think the kelpie would need it, but it felt right to go through the old drill steps for a departure anyway. He pulled the bandoleer with weapons and the kobold net from the bag, and stowed the net in the bandoleer. He tucked his bag under the side of the rowboat for safe keeping, and quickly pulled off his jumper and shoes. Then he slung the bandoleer across his chest, returned to the railings, and slipped his legs under the lowest rail. Spray brushed his bare soles. He looked down at the Atlantic.

For a very brief moment, he felt almost afraid of the sea.

Then he saw a piece of wind shaped like a twisting horse plummet from the ship and down through the foam; and he heard a man's voice calling somewhere on deck, too close for comfort; and he slipped out under the railings, into the crashing of the waves, and the waiting world below.

THE SEAFLOOR
FROM *THE SEA AND ITS CITIZENS*, DRAFT MANUSCRIPT

From above, the sea is a blank expanse of ever-changing water. For many creatures of the surface and the shallows, this *is* the sea. But there is another world, the seafloor, with its own citizens. Here there are mountains and valleys, volcanos and dunes, canyons and forests and plains.

In places, the seabed splits open, and releases boiling water from beneath the earth. This water carries minerals, some of which fall and form long, thin chimneys. These are known to the Weard as 'smokers'.

Notably, the minerals include fresh silver. This can be drawn out in greater quantities and filtered by using the skin of a kobold, the silver-eating hobgoblin found near underground silver ore on land. The skin will seal tightly around the captured silver, but will release it within a day or so.

The smokers have their own alien citizens, feeding on their plumes, living independently of plants and sunlight. The waters of this tiny kingdom are considered hostile, and the merfolk will not swim there.

14

The strength of the waves took Dylan by surprise: he had never been small in a stormy sea. For a moment he was locked below the surface in their tumbling roll and drag, turned over and round and over, the sound of roaring water filling the world . . .

Then the kelpie nudged him out of the waves and into deeper water, scattering fish and bubbles. Dylan knew it must have been the kelpie, because the nudge felt something like a warm muzzle, and something like a cold draught; and as he drifted down, something that was both a back and a gust of wind came below him and scooped him up.

He groped for a neck, and tried to adjust to a riding position. This was easier said than done. Dylan had never ridden a normal, tangible horse, and the kelpie rippled confusingly under his touch, and had taken on the colour of the water – only darker – like a shadow suspended in the sea. He was uneasily balanced, but there was no time to perfect his technique. As soon as he was more or less seated, the kelpie pointed itself downwards, and dived.

Water rushed past Dylan. The dawn cast everything in

blue, and the first rays of light fell through the water in swirling shafts, glittering on busy scales as fish swarmed around them. But fish and water and light all burst aside for the shadow-horse as it plunged downwards.

They descended at a sickening speed. The blue water turned to grey, and the light was no longer a solid thing, and the flashing shoals thinned. Dylan felt a stab of panic. His wyrm eyes were much better than this, and he used to be able to sense movement in the water too, which had been like a second sight. Now, he was losing vision fast. How would he navigate the rift wall in the dark?

It was less than a minute before the world was black.

He felt the kelpie straighten out from its dive and begin to swim forwards instead, apparently still sure of the way. Dylan was blind and lost. He clung on, and his heart pounded at every pincer-click or keening cry that floated to him across the dark. When he saw lights ahead, he thought at first it was a cluster of some deep-sea creatures, flashing their other-worldly blue-green lights. But these lights stayed absolutely still, which was strange. And as the kelpie swam on, they grew larger and whiter, and Dylan gradually understood what he was seeing: merlights.

Closer still, the lights began to illuminate the water. Here, Dylan could make out the ring of merfolk.

He had never seen them in such numbers. They were shadows here, each its own undulating shape, according to whether the disease had taken legs or arms or snake-like torso, left or right or both; and the shapes were made stranger by the weapons that protruded from bandoleers and belts and spiked silver headwear. It took an effort of will to remember that these armoured shadows were humans and allies, and not to tug back against the kelpie's neck as it plunged forward into the circle of light.

Only once they were surrounded by the folk and their silver did the kelpie slow. From the way it rippled beneath him like ragged breathing, Dylan understood that it was exhausted. It landed with a soft puff of sand on the seafloor.

The circle of folk held their hands out in greeting. Dylan returned the gesture, and discovered that his tired arms were shaking.

By the merlight, he could make out the uneven basalt floor of the Ridge. At the edge of the light, the sudden scar of darkness could only be the valley.

The kelpie trotted towards the valley's edge, then paused. One of the merfolk swam over to them: a woman. She was scaled from the neck downwards on her right side. With her left hand, she handed Dylan a merlight.

He didn't know the sign for thank you. He just clutched his free hand to his chest as Caspian had done, in what he hoped was an all-purpose gesture of respect. She did not return it; only bowed her head, and returned to the circle. The folk drifted into a new formation over the valley, and those carrying bows and arrows drew their weapons, and pointed them downward. They waited.

From somewhere unthinkably distant, a whale cried out in the dark. Nothing replied.

Dylan felt the kelpie tense. He clung on with one arm now, the other holding the lamp. Then he slid forward against its neck once more, as it kicked against the seabed, rose up, and dived.

The water in the valley was icy cold. The kelpie moved more slowly, letting Dylan scan the rock of the valley wall as it passed within his beam of light. The landscape looked different now that he was so small; he could not make up his mind whether he knew where they were.

In the end, he heard the smokers before he saw them. The sound started as a rumble, but as they descended, it grew to a world-shaking roar. Then came the black smoke-like plumes blooming in his beam of light, forming pillars far taller than he was, so that it was still some way down before he reached the tubes of the smokers themselves, spindle-thin and vastly taller than trees. They sprouted from a broad ledge set into the valley wall. The kelpie landed there, and Dylan dismounted.

A white crab scuttled over his foot. The creatures of the smokers were sunless and blind. This one clicked curiously to itself at the alien it had found, then hurried on its way, over to a carpet of limp white tube-worms with fleshy red heads. These writhed, and Dylan had the uneasy sense that they were disturbed by his arrival, and seeking him out. He took a step back in disgust.

There was a half-nudge, half-breeze at his back, urging him on. He set down the lamp, and unhooked the net before taking it up again with his free hand. He looked at the kelpie, but it folded its shadow legs firmly under itself and sat down: Dylan had the distinct impression it was shaking its head.

Fair enough. This part was his job. He kicked off, and

drifted up from the ledge towards the spreading smoke, and the smokers' spout.

The water around the smokers cooled rapidly, but at the very rim of the spout, the heat was sudden and deadly. Dylan kept a cautious distance; the long handle of the net was designed to avoid the risk of boiling alive. It took him a few tries to latch on, and once in his frustration he swam too close and felt a sudden warning burst of heat. But at last it took, and the red flesh of the kobold skin sealed itself, and began to inflate like a ravenous heart.

Then all he had to do was wait.

There was a twinge of pain at his rib, and his heart tumbled over like a wave.

He only needed a minute longer – maybe less – the little kobold skin was a good one, and was filling itself with gusto. But he couldn't unseal it before it was finished – not without losing the silver. He hung on.

The pain came at his wrist next, and it took determination to hold on to the handle of the net, and keep it steady. But surely any moment now, the kobold would be finished . . .

A much sharper tug made him writhe and cry out silently into the sea, letting a gush of cold valley-water into his lungs. He dropped the light, which plummeted into the black below. But just then the net unsealed itself with a satisfied *pop*, and Dylan wasted no time; he thrusted upwards, away from the ghost-world and the black smoke, heading for the star-like lights above.

In his panic he forgot the kelpie, until a rush of wind under him propelled him upwards at a sickening speed. He clung on with one shaking arm, stowing the net safely in his bandoleer with the other.

He was in the edges of the folks' light when the hag caught up to him, shooting itself straight towards his neck from his right. From the folk above, a silver arrow came and sent it spinning and hissing away, missing Dylan himself by half an inch as the kelpie pulled them left.

Then they were over the lip of the valley, and the merfolk closed ranks, and Dylan was borne upwards in a tight circle of glittering silver blades.

The pain from the hagflesh was blinding now. He heard, more than saw, the screeching attacks of the hag itself, which threw itself time and time again at the circle of weapons. The folk formed a formidable wall, but the hag was fast, and used its razor-mouth to tear at human and scaled flesh. More than once it succeeded in breaking through the ranks, and had to be whisked away from Dylan's side with a second to spare.

The water grew blue again, but Dylan's eyes were filling with black like the plumes of smokers, and the pain was white hot now, and it was hard to remember which way was up, and so much easier to sink down . . .

He slid from the kelpie. For a moment there was a confusion of rippling flanks and water and flashes of silver weapons. Two arms at his waist bore him the last fathoms to the surface; he barely knew, then, where he was.

The marbled swirl of surface waves was in sight when the hag made its last lunge. A dagger was thrown. The hag swerved, and with its tail sent the dagger against the soft belly of the man supporting Dylan; he crumpled in pain, and let go.

Then there was a shock of foam and cold air, and Dylan was above the waves.

The shock cleared his brain, a little. The merfolk did not break the surface; below Dylan, the kelpie found him again and bore him forwards, towards the distant safety of the ship ahead, leaving the horror below behind. It was almost finished.

And then Dylan saw, to his right, red-stained waves. As he watched, a figure was tossed up again like a log. A merfolk man: the crumpled man caught by the dagger.

Or rather, not a man – not quite. Somewhere between a man and a boy.

Caspian.

15

The kelpie was moving at speed towards the ship. It held Dylan above the surface now, clear of the hag, which gave him the strange airy sense that he rode on the foam of the sea.

He craned over his shoulder, watching as Caspian disappeared and reappeared among the sparkling waves, waiting for one of the other merfolk to emerge and claim him. But the merfolk were pragmatic, and not always merciful; and there was a long journey home to be managed. Caspian continued to dance limply in the waves, and nobody appeared.

'Wait!' called Dylan, tugging at the kelpie's neck. 'We have to go back!'

The kelpie whinnied its refusal, and kept bucking forwards.

'Please!' Dylan yelled. And when it ignored him, he threw himself from its back, and began to swim for the prone figure in the waves. With a swoop the kelpie was under him again, lifting him to safety, and galloping with a reluctant snort towards Caspian. For a second there was nothing under Dylan as the kelpie dived; then it re-emerged with both of them on its back, Caspian draped over sideways so that Dylan had to lean forward and hang on to him to keep him safe. Then they were off, bucking and rolling over the waves, racing for the aft of the SS *Rose Marie* as she forged ahead across the Atlantic.

Caspian was not conscious. It was hard to tell if he was breathing, among the confusing rolling movement of horse and waves.

Dylan's heart sank to see that someone was staring out at them from the aft of the ship, but then rose again on seeing it was Uncle Firth, watching them arrive with an expression of horror. Dylan realised his own skin was streaked with Caspian's blood, but there was no way to explain over the crashing of the waves, or to ask Uncle Firth why he had left his post at Rose's door.

He shut his eyes as the kelpie reared back, and leaped over the rails on to the deck.

There was a clatter somewhere between hooves and wind, then Dylan felt himself lowered to the floor. When he opened his eyes, he was kneeling on the tarred wood, Caspian beside him, the kelpie nothing but a tired breath of wind at the nape of his neck.

Uncle Firth had stepped back from the spray, but now he leaped into action. He pulled off his coat, and grabbed Dylan's blanket; with the ends of his jumper wrapped around his hands against the sting of salt water, he was covering the unconscious Caspian in a hasty bundle, pushing his tail-end into a coil to make him smaller. As he worked, he muttered, 'Very lucky – deckhands here just a few minutes ago – just have to hope no one was looking from that middle bit of the deck . . .'

Dylan only watched uselessly, mind blank.

'Put it on,' said Uncle Firth, thrusting his jumper at him. Dylan obeyed. Uncle Firth untied the signal knot and put Dylan's bag over his shoulder, then said, 'Take the feet'. Dylan obeyed again, and they hoisted Caspian up, the bandoleer and net tucked on top of him under the blanket and coat; then they were hurrying up the steps with their heavy load.

Dylan's clothes covered up most of the blood smeared on him, and the blanket full of Caspian was helpfully non-human-shaped with his tail curled in. Still, when they saw officers scrubbing the deck starboard, they quickly backtracked and went round the ship on the freshly-scrubbed port side. Dylan had no idea what story he would offer for his soaked appearance and the strange bundle if they were stopped.

Port side was quiet, and they arrived at the fo'c'sle without incident, although above them two officers stood on the deck – thankfully, looking out to sea. Silently, Dylan transferred Caspian's weight to Uncle Firth, and opened the door for him. They had just slipped inside when the officer called Bill turned to look at Dylan.

'Hello!' he called – more as an exclamation of surprise than a greeting. 'You're soaked!'

'Yeah,' said Dylan. 'Enormous wave – got sprayed.'

Bill looked at him. 'When?'

'Just now,' said Dylan vaguely. 'Going to change into something warm' – and he slipped quickly through the door, praying that Bill would not bother to give this too much thought. Inside, he quickly took his half of the weight again.

'Bathroom?' said Dylan.

Uncle Firth nodded. 'Probably best.'

Dylan was thankful that there were no other landman passengers on board – Rose was a different problem, but that would have to wait. They went into the little bathroom, and set Caspian on the floor. Dylan turned the bath taps, and salt water began to gush in. He could no longer feel the kelpie; if it was there, it was keeping still. Behind him, Uncle Firth began to unwrap the bundle.

'Oh,' he said softly.

Dylan turned to see. Caspian's side was torn open, right across the strangely neat divide between his healthy flesh and his scaled skin. He was as pale as the sunless creatures of the smoker, and if it hadn't been for his ragged breaths, Dylan would not have known he was alive.

'I'll get the woundwort,' said Uncle Firth. 'Stay with him.'

Dylan knelt at Caspian's head. He wanted to reach out, to help in some way, but he was afraid to touch the limp body in case he hurt it more. He kept his eyes fixed on the rise and fall of Caspian's lungs, as though sheer will power could keep them moving.

Uncle Firth returned with the medicine tin, handed Dylan voleskin to cut for bandages, and began working on a poultice.

'Do you think he'll live?' said Dylan.

'If it's a flesh wound, I'd have thought so,' said Uncle Firth. 'Lots of organs round there. I don't know how to tell what's been damaged.'

Dylan's hands shook as he cut the bandage. 'I know him,'

he said, 'sort of. He was the one who I met at home in the firth, before we left.'

Uncle Firth made an interested noise, but was mostly focused on his poultice.

'His name's Caspian,' said Dylan.

Uncle Firth nodded. 'Well, Caspian,' he said, 'may the moon keep you.' And he leaned over the body, poultice in hand, to tend to the wound.

Once or twice while he worked, Caspian's eyelids fluttered, and he moaned a little. But he didn't wake. Dylan lowered him, bandaged up tightly like a swaddled baby, into the half-filled bath. Then they both knelt, and looked down at him uncertainly.

'Right,' said Uncle Firth, 'that's all we can do for him. Now we wait.'

Dylan nodded. 'He was defending me from the hag. It was down there, at the end. What happened to Rose?'

'I'm sorry. She'd left her room – the door was ajar. I looked all over, I didn't know what to do. I found your things and I just waited for you. River, I'm so happy you're alive. And you got the silver?'

'Yes.' It was only now occurring to Dylan that technically, this had been a success. It didn't *feel* like a success. He looked over at the bandoleer, with its precious cargo. 'The kobold will still be sealed – it should open itself soon.'

'Well *done*,' said Uncle Firth. 'Oh, Dylan – I'm so relieved.'

Dylan nodded. They looked at each other, uncle and nephew: so alike, on the outside.

Then Dylan crumpled, and he was hugging his uncle like a small child, face buried in his shoulder; and Uncle Firth clung tightly back, and they shook against each other like pieces of seaweed in a storm.

They agreed to watch Caspian in shifts. Uncle Firth sent Dylan for dried chara cakes from the cabin, since the ship's breakfast was long since over. Dylan didn't feel hungry, but Uncle Firth insisted.

Rose was in the corridor when he came out, clearly waiting to speak with him. When the door opened, she could see straight into the bathtub behind him, where Caspian lay in bandages stained with blooms of blood.

Her face fell open in horror. It seemed to be genuine. The look in her eyes took Dylan straight back to an unwanted memory: *There's been another attack. Mac Purley's little girl.*

'Oh! Who – is he . . . ? A *mermaid*? Oh God, it looks bad.'

Dylan shut the bathroom door, and tried to push past her. She put a hand on his arm to stop him, and she was all parted lips and wide eyes, and it was infuriating to discover that even now he knew what she was, his heart still beat faster.

'Salt off!' He shook off her hand.

'You're wet! Have you been in the sea? Are you still going later?'

'I'll be myself next time,' he said. 'You're too late.' He swerved, but she moved to block him, all feigned puzzlement.

'What—' she began.

'Stop it,' Dylan half yelled. 'You can drop the temptress act and the beautiful . . . this' – he gestured at her vaguely, to indicate that all of this false form was beautiful. 'You've made yourself very alluring, well done. You got me. But I know what you are now. And you're too late.' And this time when he dodged past her he was quick enough, and he had his cabin door open and slammed shut again before she could gather a reply.

The knocking on the door went on for a long time this time, and she was shouting through the door too, demanding explanations, muddled in with equally fierce demands to know if he was all right. He sat on the bunk with his fingers in his ears, willing her to leave.

It occurred to him, as her shouts died down to half-hearted repetitions of his name, that if by any chance she *wasn't* the hag, he had just yelled at a normal girl about how beautiful and alluring he found her. This thought was too humiliating to contemplate. And it wasn't worth contemplating, anyway: he was not really in any doubt.

As though in answer, the kelpie shimmered into man form. It was lying on the bunk above Uncle Firth's, curled up in the foetal position. It looked down at Dylan earnestly, and croaked, 'Danger. Dylan Pade. Hag.'

'Yes,' said Dylan. He felt, suddenly, very tired. 'I know.'

16

For several hours Caspian didn't wake, and the kobold stayed sealed shut, and Dylan waited. After breakfast and enforced rest he took over from Uncle Firth and watched Caspian, who breathed more evenly now, and seemed a shade less pale – but did not open his eyes.

After what might have been minutes or hours, Uncle Firth was back, insisting it was his turn.

'You need proper rest, Dylan,' he said, when Dylan protested. 'There's still a huge task ahead of you. Go, I'll watch.'

Dylan knew he couldn't rest, so he went up on deck, climbing the ladder up over their cabins to watch the waves from the front of the ship. He was warmly wrapped in one of Grandpa Willig's spare jumpers, which was snug in its slightly-too-small-ness, and had the musty sweet smell of Grandpa's boat. The Atlantic was a deep chill blue now, jagged with waves. Dylan felt very keenly what a small and soft thing he was.

He had, of course, not been the one to hurt Caspian. That didn't stop the old panic coming back, as once again he waited while a life hung in the balance. He tried to think instead about what he must do next, when the kobold opened. But this was unreal to him; he remembered little of his sea-life, so anything that was going to happen to his sea-self felt only distantly relevant to his own concerns. The panic over Caspian, on the other hand, was immediate. The hagflesh throbbed too, but that wasn't important, now that he had the silver.

Deckhands came and went. Dylan didn't look around when footsteps approached, until a polite 'Good day' announced the presence of Captain Groves.

Dylan turned. Captain Groves seemed very small too. They were two tiny helpless little people, bobbing up and down hideously on the huge sea.

'I am informed,' said the captain, 'that you were seen earlier very wet. And I have a separate report from the watch on the bridge that you and your uncle were carrying a large bundle of fabric around the deck. I have come to enquire if there was an incident I should know about.'

It was an effort to care enough about this to lie. 'I was splashed by a big wave,' Dylan tried. 'Our coats and things got soaked – that's what we were carrying.'

'The man who saw you close-to was of the opinion that you were rather too wet for this hypothesis,' said Captain Groves, with all his polite indifference.

Dylan shrugged. 'Well – that's what happened.' He didn't think he needed a more elaborate lie. The captain was clearly questioning him out of a weak sense of obligation, which seemed likely to fizzle out soon.

'I see,' said the captain. He paused, calculating. 'Some

of my men are somewhat fanciful,' he said. 'I apologise for intruding on you. But I must also impress upon you the need for safety on board the ship. In future,' he added – and now he sounded pompously official, with the definite air of someone doing their best to find some kind of firm point, 'I must ask you to keep a safe distance from the rails when the sea is choppy.'

'Yes,' said Dylan. 'I will.'

'Please tell your uncle.'

Dylan nodded solemnly.

'Well – good day, then,' said Captain Groves.

'Yes. Bye,' said Dylan. And Groves went trotting away to the ladder, then was out of sight again, leaving Dylan to sea and sky.

Dylan was reminded, somehow, of Grandpa watching him go – letting him go. The world outside his cottage and his family was full of a terrible indifference. It was only him and Uncle Firth now who knew or cared what needed to be done by the Weard, and what that meant for the people who had to hold the office – for Dylan alone, now. He was going to have to get used to people only half seeing him, only talking to finish a duty or fill the time.

Caspian had been different, of course. Caspian had helped.

The panic rose up again, and grasped at Dylan's throat.

When Dylan went back below decks, the ship was rocking on the waves, and for the first time on board he found he moved a little unsteadily. He went to the room first: the kobold, hidden inside one of their cases, was still sealed. Then he went to the bathroom.

To his astonishment, Caspian was awake. He was very pale, but enthusiastically consuming chara cakes.

'Oh!' said Dylan. Relief made him almost laugh. 'You're awake!'

Caspian did the merfolk equivalent of beaming at him, eyes crinkling in delight. 'Thanks to you,' he said.

'Oh, no. *You* saved *me*. Are you going to – is it . . . ?' And it seemed indelicate, somehow, to ask Caspian if he was going to live; so he directed his unfinished question at Uncle Firth.

'It's looking very positive,' said Uncle Firth. 'Caspian can eat – nothing seems to be damaged, internally. We'll need to keep dressing the wound, and I'm afraid the pain will last a while yet, but I'd expect a full recovery.'

'That's brilliant,' said Dylan, grinning at Caspian.

'Yes,' said Caspian. 'It is.'

Uncle Firth stood, stretching to ease his back. 'I might get some dinner,' he said, 'if you're all right to stay a while, Dylan?'

'Yes, of course.'

'I'll see if I can bring you something from the mess – if not we can change places in a mo. Did you check on the kobold already?'

'Mm – nothing yet.'

Uncle Firth nodded. 'See you in a bit then. See you, Caspian.'

'Thank you, Firth Pade,' said Caspian, clutching his arm to his chest with difficulty; and when Uncle Firth had gone, he said, 'He has been generous. I owe you both a great debt.'

'Like I said, you saved *me* back there. We're even.' Dylan

settled on the floor between the tub and the wall. From here, Caspian was a little floating head above the tub, which made him look oddly child-like. Every time the ship rose and fell, the water in the bath splooshed gently.

Dylan wasn't sure how to ask his next question, but he thought he ought to try, in case Caspian wanted to talk about it. 'I wasn't sure if the other folk were coming back for you,' he said delicately. 'I hope we didn't interfere too soon . . .'

Caspian shook his head. 'They would not have come,' he said.

'Is that – normal?'

'Yes. They did not carry what I needed – they could not have tended to me until we were within our own waters. I would have died on the way, and my bleeding in open water would have endangered everyone.'

He seemed so calm about this that Dylan couldn't help protesting. 'But what were you supposed to do? Just stay there and die?'

Caspian showed no sign of distress. 'It is usual to find a sunken ship if you have the strength,' he said, 'to ensure a peaceful death.'

'You mean wreck-water?'

'I have heard your word for it, yes.'

Dylan was flabbergasted. The water around wrecks was a death sentence. It was mixed in with the spirit lost by the drowned, and would greedily enter into any living flesh it could find. This sometimes kept the almost-dead alive for a time, animated by the spirit, but in the end it would kill its host.

'Why would you *do* that?' he said.

Caspian half moved towards a shrug, and immediately winced in regret. 'There are many predators that will come if you bleed in open ocean. But they will not enter wreck-water. There are better and worse deaths.' He looked at Dylan earnestly then, and Dylan had the impression he was making up his mind whether to say something else. Then the ship lurched on an especially large wave, and his face spasmed with pain. Dylan quickly half rose.

'Are you all right? Can I help?'

'I – am well,' said Caspian, breathing unevenly. 'The waves can be discomforting. It is strange to be above them.'

'Isn't it?' said Dylan. 'It sort of throws your insides off balance.'

'They feel like good strong waves. It will be fresh in the shallows.'

'Yes. And it'll be silvering now.' Dylan's flashes of sea-self memories often featured the silvering hour at dusk, when blue faded to grey and bright fish turned to shadows.

Caspian gave Dylan one of his earnest, considering looks. 'Forgive me,' he said, 'but it is hard for me to understand how you could choose exile from the Sea.'

Dylan shrugged. 'I'm undoing it. I've got the silver.'

'But you were willing.'

'I put it off for a long time,' Dylan said. 'But I've always thought about it.' He didn't want to go into his reasons right now, so he turned his face to a smile instead, and said, 'And the land's nice too, you know.'

'I am sure it is beautiful,' said Caspian, 'but it is so little of the world. And even that little is broken into pieces – you cannot cross it freely. And movement looks so hard and slow!' He did little plod-plod movements with his fists in imitation of walking – Dylan couldn't actually see this, but it was clear from the splashing of the water and the plodding weary face Caspian pulled. 'No floating!' he said. 'No diving! No currents to ride!'

'I've often thought flying might be even better,' Dylan suggested.

Caspian shook his head, with the certainty of someone who has had this argument before. 'What is there to see in the sky? Flying up into wider and wider loneliness. Where are the meadows and forests and valleys and mountains in the sky?'

Dylan raised his hands in mock-surrender. 'Indisputable,' he said. 'The sea wins.' Then he added, 'Was it a long time ago, then – when you – left the rivers, when you went to sea?' It seemed rude to say, 'when you got sick'. Dylan wasn't sure if the merfolk thought of themselves as sick.

'I do not know my age,' said Caspian. This made him thoughtful again, the sudden animation gone. 'It seems to me that I have been what I am for a very long time.'

'Do you ever see your family?'

'The Sea is mother and father,' said Caspian. He had the air of someone quoting: a shared merfolk creed, perhaps. Dylan thought this seemed unbearably sad, and there was a silence that went on slightly too long, so he cast around for something else to say.

'The kelpie thinks the hag's on board,' he said, 'with a human form.'

'Your uncle told me,' said Caspian. 'He wished to know my thoughts.'

'And what are your thoughts?'

'I know little of hags, but I would trust a kelpie,' said Caspian. 'I am told that they see the future only partially, but what they see is true.'

'That's what I've been saying,' said Dylan. He leaned his head back against the cool metal wall and shut his eyes, as the ship took another exceptional wave. 'It had better be true,' he said, 'or I've been very rude for no reason.' He decided against sharing that he had told her she was beautiful and alluring – he had actually used the word *alluring* out loud – because just thinking about it made him feel like hitting his head very hard against the wall.

'I would trust a kelpie,' Caspian repeated. 'And you have the silver now?'

'Yes. We're just waiting for the kobold to unseal.'

'Do you know what you must do, when you are restored?'

'Just get the others out, for now – my family and the others – we can come back to bind the nál when they've recovered.'

Caspian was watching him, head cocked, all earnest interest again. 'You do not seem afraid.'

'Not about that bit,' Dylan agreed. 'My sea-self feels so different, I don't really get afraid about the sea. It's not bravery or anything – I'm *terrified* about what happens afterwards.'

'Afterwards?'

'If anything goes wrong. I'm afraid of failing, of losing somebody . . . I keep checking the blood, in case one of them's gone.' He hesitated – it was bad form to push merfolk on something they didn't want to speak about – but he asked, 'You said my family mean something to you. What happened?'

Caspian watched him for a long moment; the bath sploosh-splooshed in the quiet. Dylan waited respectfully. Then Caspian seemed to make up his mind – but when he spoke, it wasn't to answer the question.

'There is something I must tell you,' said Caspian at last. 'The folk did not wish you to know.'

Dylan sat up straight, gut clenching. 'What? Do you have news? About my family? What is it?'

But Caspian was still stuck on his internal grappling. 'There was a binding vote against telling you,' he said. 'The argument was that you must go to the Sargasso, and not endanger yourself. But my misgivings . . .'

'Caspian, what is it?'

Caspian hesitated, then made up his mind. 'It is news of your sisters,' he said.

'Yes?' Dylan found he had knelt, and was gripping the bathtub.

'They have escaped the nál –'

'*What?*'

'– but they are weak. They have gone to choose a better death.'

For the first time since he had known Caspian, Dylan felt the familiar desire to scream at the vague mystical proclamations of the merfolk. 'What in salt does that mean?'

'It is as we spoke of,' said Caspian, seeming to shrink

slightly under Dylan's glare. 'They are sheltering from the pull of the nál. They are in wreck-water.'

'What? But they'll die there!'

The ship soared on the largest wave yet, and Caspian moaned a little, sudden and sharp, then breathed in raggedly. 'Yes,' he agreed, 'soon they will. They may yet live. And you may be able to help them, in your other form. It is risky.' He shut his eyes. 'It was a binding vote. But I think it is right that you choose.'

WRECK-WATER

FROM *THE SEA AND ITS CITIZENS*, DRAFT MANUSCRIPT

Where landmen drown in great numbers, the water can become thick with their lost spirit. This creates the liquid spirit known as wreck-water.

Wreck-water wants flesh to live inside. It will enter any body, living or dead, and mimic the functions of life. This can delay death, for somebody already near-dying, but it will eventually be fatal.

Many creatures avoid wreck-water, and currents are powerless to move it, so it can provide a sanctuary for the hunted. However, this is a desperate measure. No one should stay beyond a single tide-turn.

17

The folk were wrong. There was no question of leaving his sisters in the wreck. Dylan could bring them safely to the ship, and go on to find his parents, all before any of them had to die. He was sure of this with the unarguable, slightly-hysterical certainty of someone who needs something to be true, because all other options are unacceptable.

Caspian described the wreck, and Dylan knew exactly where he meant; he had seen it from a distance, although he had never been allowed to swim too close. It was less than two decades old, and the fog of the wreck-water there was especially vivid. It had always intrigued the Pade children. For one birthday, Meriel had bought Tor a book about the ship called *Titanic*, and they had all read it until the pages fell out.

It had been bound for New York, like the SS *Rose Marie*. They would pass close by. And Dylan would be himself again.

Dusk fell, and Dylan checked their course. They were about five hours from the wreck. For something to do with the time, he eked out painfully precise sums, pinpointing as closely as he could the time he expected to be nearest the wreck – although for his sea-self, a little distance either side would be nothing. He would prefer to go down as soon as he was himself, even if it was early. Better to be doing something.

But for now, he went below decks, and back to the bathroom where Caspian and Uncle Firth waited.

They had moved the kobold into the bathroom, partly to keep an eye on both kobold and Caspian at once, and partly because the kelpie kept accidentally turning into wind and knocking it over. The kelpie was exhausted – or at least, Dylan assumed that was the problem. It seemed to have trouble controlling its form, and in all its forms it was limp and fragile, shutting its eyes when it had them. It had nodded assurances when asked if it was all right, and shaken its head and sighed when asked if it needed anything. The sighs were the dangerous part; it tended to dissolve into a gust of wind without warning.

So now the kelpie lay tucked under the covers on the bunk above Dylan's, just about holding on to its man form, while Uncle Firth and Caspian and the kobold skin cluttered up the little bathroom. Dylan didn't know where Rose was. He almost wished she would loiter in the corridor again, just so that he could know; but as he returned below decks, the corridor was empty.

In the bathroom, the kobold was still sealed shut.

With four hours to go, it continued to be shut. It remained shut with three hours to go, and singularly failed to unshut itself with two. With one hour to go, Dylan had begun to lose hope.

'You can turn back for them in wyrm form,' said Uncle

Firth. 'Sailing a few nautical miles past them while you wait is neither here nor there.'

Dylan nodded, but he carried on staring at the little kobold skin, praying that this wouldn't be necessary. To sail away from his sisters would feel like a betrayal, and at this stage, that might be one feeling too many.

And then the kobold unsealed.

He had never actually seen it happen before. There was a pop, like a cork from a bottle, and the whole thing trembled gently. Then – slowly, gracefully – it stretched itself upwards, and unfurled. The silver inside was liquid and thick, like shining cream; it would not become a solid lump of silver until it was decanted.

'*Oh*,' said Uncle Firth softly. Caspian tried to sit a little higher to see more clearly, then winced, and lay back. He seemed to be healing remarkably well, though, considering. And now the kobold had opened.

Uncle Firth looked at Dylan, and from the look in his eyes, Dylan feared a helpful encouraging speech. He didn't want to pause for the length of a speech; it was better not to look at this moment too clearly or for too long. It was time to become himself again. He rolled up a sleeve, and plunged his hand and half his forearm into the waiting silver.

He cried out a little as the hagflesh writhed and twisted from its roots under his skin. There was a sharp pinching, as though it was hanging on to his veins in desperation. He gritted his teeth, and kept his wrist in the silver until the pinch slackened and the writhing fell still.

He withdrew his arm, dripping rivulets of silver. His skin

was thick with it. It looked as though a metal hand had been cast with improbable perfection: the wrinkles of the knuckles, the lines of the cuticles. The criss-crossed skin of the hagflesh, still embedded in his wrist.

'Is it still feeding?' asked Caspian.

'I'm not sure,' said Dylan. With his other hand, he picked up some discarded voleskin from the making of Caspian's bandages. He soaked it in the silver, lifted his jumper and shirt, and pressed the silvery rag to the flesh. Again, it writhed horribly, this time squirming deep in the marrow of his lowest left rib. Again, he kept the silver there until it fell still.

But it was still very much attached.

'Let's try you in some water,' suggested Uncle Firth. 'See if the sea-self's stirring . . .'

So Dylan plunged his silver-free arm into the bath, the water cold against human skin. He watched his hand; the other two watched his face.

Nothing strained against his skin at the touch of water. Nothing rattled against his bones.

Dylan kept staring stupidly at his hand, waiting. This couldn't be the end of it. Fresh sea-silver was incredibly potent. How could it have failed?

He scrabbled at the hagflesh with his good hand. It was just as embedded as ever.

'Right,' said Uncle Firth. 'There must be more to the cure, then. We'll go over what we know of the Lore, and devise some experiments . . .'

'There's no time,' said Dylan. He was standing, his mind racing through the possibilities, fighting not to give in to panic.

He didn't know what he would do about the nál, now, but he could direct his sisters to the *Rose Marie* at least – if he lost this moment, he was in danger of going home with nobody.

He checked the watch on his good wrist, then took it off in preparation. 'If I'm travelling at human speed,' he said, 'I have to go right now.'

'What can you do as you are?'

'Fetch the twins, get them to the ship. They just have to follow the nál's drag, if I can tell them . . .'

'The hag—' said Uncle Firth and Caspian together.

'I know!' bellowed Dylan, unfairly enraged with his friends, wanting to rip the awful hagflesh from his body even if it meant tearing away his own hand and heart. 'I am aware! It's hard to forget when it's eating you all the salting time.'

Uncle Firth had stood too, but Dylan was already out into the corridor, storming to their cabin, slamming open the door. The cabin looked empty. 'Kelpie!' he yelled.

To his right, the air sighed.

'I need to talk to you.'

The air became a pale man with magnificent resignation.

'I'm going in the sea. Can you travel?'

The kelpie's dark eyes grew wider and darker, and it shook its head with great emphasis: it seemed to mean simultaneously *No, I cannot* and *No, you must not*.

'Fine,' said Dylan, not needing a silent windy repeat of Uncle Firth and Caspian's protestations. He wheeled round to find his uncle hovering behind him, hair all hedgehogged in alarm, eyes all softness. 'Dylan—'

'Where's Rose?' he said. He pushed past Uncle Firth and

shoved at Rose's cabin door. It was unlocked, and the cabin was empty. Dimly, he noticed that there was a bright coverlet, and some pictures pinned to the wall: an oddly human-looking room. 'Find her if you can,' he said. 'I have to go.'

'Dylan, there'll be a way, we just have to keep trying . . .'

Dylan was already marching down the corridor. 'Meriel and Tor are here right now, Firth.'

With a skittish dart, Uncle Firth dodged in front of Dylan, blocking the door. 'I won't let you, Dylan.'

'I am the Weard of the Sea,' Dylan roared.

'You are also my sister's precious child.'

Dylan looked at Uncle Firth, wide-eyed and wild, and suddenly he saw it all in a new light: all his uncle's worried, dithering concern, so almost-like his family's love. *My sister's precious child.* 'I'm not Auntie Isla,' he said coldly. 'This isn't some sort of redemption for you. Move . . .' – and Dylan reached for the door, and Uncle Firth moved to stop him, and improbably they were wrestling, a sport neither of them was practised at or enthusiastic for, tumbling inexpertly against the door as they grappled at each other. Dylan half fell, his ankle twinging sharply in reproof. He felt Uncle Firth push, almost sending him to the floor. He shook himself free, and punched his uncle on the nose.

'*Nghhh*,' said Uncle Firth, in a mixture of pain and surprise.

Blindly, Dylan shoved him to the floor, and heaved at the outside door. The thud behind him suggested Uncle Firth might have hit a wall on his way down. Too bad. He broke out on to the deck at a slightly-hobbling run.

It was raining, and the ship was soaring on enormous stormy waves. The hagflesh had begun to stir in awful revenge under Dylan's skin. He stumbled and skidded across the heaving deck, down the stairs, to the aft of the ship.

With the noise of wind and rain and waves, he didn't hear the footsteps close behind him until he stopped at the rails. He assumed it was Uncle Firth; he turned, and swore loudly on seeing Rose. Panicked, he began tugging off his jumper, as though he might still be able to lose her if he got in the sea fast enough. The silvered hand was clumsy.

Rose was talking, but he could only hear snatches over the storm. '. . . heard yelling,' she explained. '. . . see if I could help . . . your hand . . . doing? Are you going in the sea?'

'Salt off!' said Dylan, climbing the rails. He didn't look at her.

'What?' she yelled. He felt her move closer behind him, and belatedly his brain registered that she couldn't possibly be outpaced at this point. It would be better to fight her here on deck, in her human form.

He didn't turn and fight her, but he didn't dive either. He seemed to be frozen. 'Salt,' he said, more loudly. 'Off.'

She climbed up beside him, stopping a cautious rung below his, but bringing her face level. Her black curls were alive in the raging wind; she had never looked less human, and where she brushed against him it felt electric. 'Salt . . . ? I don't know what that means,' she said. 'I don't understand what you think I've done . . . I have a right to know . . .'

Something unlocked at last in Dylan, and he finally reached out to wrestle her to the ground – knock her out if he had to. Her eyes widened as he gripped her shoulders, and she responded by leaning towards him, eyes alight, in a way that did not feel at all like fighting; but as she leaned she slipped on the wet rails, and her weight fell against him; and then there was an almighty heave forward from the ship as it plunged on the crest of a mountainous wave, just as they were both rocking off balance . . .

For one frozen moment they seemed to teeter over the edge of the rails, as though they might still choose to fall in either direction; as though the invisible forces that pushed and pulled them were only suggestions, and they could change their minds.

And then the spell broke. They tumbled over the edge, falling exactly as universal laws demanded, into the raging waves below.

18

At night, the sea is black from top to bottom.

In the blackness it was hard for Dylan to judge how fast he was falling. By the time he had recovered from the shock, he had already left the frenzy of the shallows, and the water around him was heavy and cold.

Sinking is slower than falling. The water lowered him gently, cradling him, stirring against him when something unseen moved nearby. His body pulsed with loud, slow-pounding heartbeats, his skin alert and prickling – waiting for the hag.

A tentacle trailed across his chest, and his whole body lurched with panic. But it was just a curious night-dweller. It trailed away again into the darkness, and another minute passed, and the hag did not appear.

When he saw the distant glow of the wreck-water, he spun to point his hands downwards, making an arrow in the water, and began to swim. Water rushed past, liquid wind against his skin. Now that the light gave him a sense of direction, he could tell that he was being pulled sideways as well as down, on a strange current – the pull of the nál. He had only just been in time, leaving the ship east of the wreck, so that it pulled him towards his goal. He was not sure he could have swum against it.

As he drew close, he could see the shadow of the wreck. The light of the wreck-water didn't grow any brighter here: it was a feeble thing, gathered like fog, fraying and reforming itself at the edges.

He was almost at that fraying edge when he saw two things at the same time. First, to his right, the slow-falling body of Rose. Further off, but closing in at speed, the hag.

There was no time to ponder the implications of this. Dylan put on a desperate burst of speed. He thrust himself into the wreck-water, ignoring the sudden bone-cold and the stillness, and the immediate dread deep in his gut. He didn't slow down until he was kneeling on the silt of the plains.

He looked up. As he had hoped, the hag had not risked the wreck-water: he had left it behind. On that front, at least, he was safe. From above, the human body of Rose drifted silently down, and came to rest on the silt several feet to his left.

She was a human. Not a hag. Dylan was dimly aware – as though the thought belonged to someone else – that this might mean he had finally killed someone.

At Rose's elbow, a sea spider investigated the new arrival. All her determined solidity was gone, and all her hunger: she had the peaceful, strangely preserved look that Dylan had seen before, on drowned landmen found on the plains. It always surprised him that they didn't collapse under all that ocean. Human frames were remarkably strong.

But perhaps the wreck-water was keeping her in half-life . . . he swam over, his movements slow and heavy here, and knelt at her side, putting two fingers to her neck. Sure enough, there was a slow, shuddering pulse. Liquid spirit re-animating a heart, opening blood vessels up against the cold, writhing into lungs, squeezing the last possible moments out of flesh. And she would have survived the pressure, since she wasn't taking in air. But how long would she last, full of the spirit of the dead?

It was in him too. The cold and quiet was seeping through his skin in much the same way rain soaks through a shirt, drenching his insides. He found he could feel the contours of his muscles and bones, the strings of his blood vessels and the budding branches of his lungs – every place that the lost spirit pressed against him. It made him heavy. His heartbeat was slow, and it was rapidly becoming harder to move.

His thoughts were slow too, and he knew he must not forget his purpose here, or forget to leave again. He pushed his body up from the silt, and with difficulty, set off at a lolloping walk.

He crossed a seabed littered with broken furniture and smashed crockery, and little heaps of watches and coins and pipes and fans and opened trunks and shoes and jewellery . . . The whole place glittered with shards of glass, which to his dazed brain looked like broken stars. Here and there, tendrils or claws waved, and scuttling creatures sent up puffs of sand. There was no sound.

He had never seen a wreck of this size up close. The ship had been broken in two like a bone: the bow ended abruptly in a vertical drop. It was covered with barnacles, and its edges dripped with enormous tendrils of rust.

Dylan walked around to the broken end. The smashed-up ruins of halved rooms towered above him.

'Meriel?' he called – realising only after he had spoken that it was peculiar to be able to open his mouth freely in this strange water. It was not a pleasant experience: it rattled his teeth in their gums. Still, he did it a second time, to call, 'Tor?'

For a moment he stood still, too blank to think what to do next. He reminded himself, under his breath, 'Meriel and Tor' – and, after a moment's fumbling in his mind to find what he'd forgotten, he added, 'Rose.' Then he pushed off from the sand and entered the wreck.

He chose a room at random. It seemed to be some sort of dining room. The remains of tables were carpeted in fat white shipworms, devouring the wood, and they were thick on the walls too. Portholes survived unmolested, and the light fixtures on the ceiling remained, looped here and there with loose festoons of electrical wiring. Silt had filled up the floor in uneven dunes. The quiet seemed deeper here, somehow.

Dylan had to fight every instinct to resist turning back. He found an opening – it was hard to know if it was an intentional doorway – and found himself in a long passage with more openings to his right. He took another room at random: this one was even thicker with sand, which half buried a brass bedstead.

Dylan's heartbeat was growing painful now, pumping in and out with slow deliberation. The strange light of the wreck-water pressed at him, and it was beginning to feel as though the foggy light was inside his eyes; the room seemed blurred. He lifted his arm – he felt muscle contract, tendons pull against bone – and rubbed his eyes. It did no good. The fog *was* on the inside, and he was losing his sight.

'Meriel, Tor,' he whispered to himself. He had a feeling he had forgotten something from this list. He looked back out into the passageway and the maze of broken ship beyond, and felt repulsed by dread; and besides, some remnant of thought urged him, a wyrm would not be in these small human rooms anyway. It didn't make sense. He was wasting time here.

After a moment's dumb hesitation, he pushed himself back out of the wreck, and up over the top, to the uppermost deck of the ship.

There.

A pile of wyrm coils lay between the snapped-off stubs of funnels. The size was breath-taking. Human-Dylan had only ever seen a wyrm from above the waves, swiftly departing, and for a moment he was horrified. He had always felt his wyrm form to be a sleek, graceful thing. These vast loops of flesh were scarred and ugly. He was looking at a monster.

Then his sluggish thoughts registered something else: amongst all these coils, he could only see one head.

He edged a little closer, and the head opened a silver eye. Dylan drifted in front of it.

'Meriel?' he tried. 'Tor?'

For one awful moment, it occurred to him that there might have been a mistake: this might be an unknown wyrm, and he, weardkin of the British Isles, might be about to die in its jaws. But then the coils shivered, and flinched, and seemed to tense . . .

And a moment later a woman crouched on the deck, curled under a curtain of long red hair. In this not-quite-water, then, she could choose to take human form. That was good. But Dylan had never seen the twins underwater as humans, and disconcertingly, he found that this erased all their telling differences. His blurring vision didn't help. Who was this? And where was his second sister?

'Is it only you here?' he asked.

The twin nodded heavily. Her eyes were searching him, but they were bright with the silvery fog, and Dylan suspected she couldn't see him.

'It's me,' he said, slightly uselessly, 'Dylan. There's a ship nearby – it's going south-west from here – if you can get us back there, carry me there, I can help you. I can't transform at the moment' – and this seemed impossibly difficult to explain in his heavy state, so he just raised his right wrist, and said, 'Hag attack.'

'Ah,' she said. Her voice was flat; if she remembered who he was, she didn't care. It was the loneliest feeling Dylan had ever known.

She coiled herself again, hiding her face, the pale skin at the top of her spine poking through the hair. One way to tell the twins apart was the habitual tilt to their spines – a little hook downwards for Meriel, like a bird feeding at low tide, and an impatient wriggling list to one side for Tor. This curled-up creature gave nothing away. Vertebrae knobbled her skin, fragile and small.

Dylan reached out to touch her shoulder, gently, as though she might float apart. 'We have to go.'

'Too dangerous.'

'You'll die if you stay here.'

'Dangerous,' she repeated.

Dylan had to fight not to give in, and curl up restfully next to her. 'You're the Weard,' he said, reaching into his memory for arguments. 'Mam and Dad are in danger. If I fail, the Weard needs two of us.'

This only made his sister's spine coil tighter, as though she could sprout a shell and hide inside it, away from weighty responsibilities. Memory burst through to Dylan. That coiled spine was Tor, perched up a tree with her head in a book. It was Meriel, in her favourite cranny of a cavern just above sea level, watching the creep of the tide, refusing to come home. It was family.

'Please,' said Dylan. '*I* need you.'

The nameless twin stayed curled up, unmoved. Dylan was all out of arguments. Should he try to drag her upwards by force? It was hard to imagine – he could barely lift him*self* in this place.

Then, red hair rippling, his sister uncoiled. Her face, when she was determined, looked like Mam's: a soldierly set of the jaw. It was the most human she had looked since he had found her.

'A ship?' she said slowly.

'Yes. You can join us. Live.'

'I carry you,' she said carefully, as though testing her memory.

'Yes. Oh! And –' a memory came to Dylan with sudden urgency – 'there's a landman girl. I don't know if she's alive – the wreck-water might have preserved her. Can you carry her too?'

Tor-Meriel nodded, incurious, concentrating. 'Take me,' she said.

'Yes. I – thank you.' Dylan was desperate with the inadequacy of this. Some part of him knew this was not how things should feel when he found his family. There was supposed to be a good, warm feeling. He couldn't quite remember what the feeling was like, but he knew that it was missing.

His one remaining sister lifted herself from the deck, her hair fanning around her in the water as she rose. 'We should leave,' she said. And she began to drift away, not looking back.

Dylan had not been held in the coils of another wyrm since he was very, very young. Distant memories stirred – the feel of the strong muscle embracing him, and the heartbeat thrumming through him, and the gentle sway as the body undulated through the sea. Next to him, Rose's body rocked and swayed in time.

A wyrm was the ultimate protector. The hag did not reappear.

Tor-Meriel needed no directions: the same current that dragged at the *Rose Marie* dragged at her. Dylan felt her muscles brace when the ship appeared overhead, furiously resisting the pull, straining to turn them upwards instead. For a moment, they hung suspended in the fight.

Then they shot upwards like the plume of a fountain.

When they burst out from the water, the screaming began.

19

The twin reassembled herself into a human as she landed on the deck, pouring herself in a swirl of silver light back into her smaller, more acceptable body. Dylan and Rose fell down heavily. From around the ship the screaming faltered as the monster vanished; on their own part of the deck, four appalled officers stared in a silence that was somehow louder. An electric light illuminated them, and gave everything a pallid glow.

Someone was kneeling at Dylan's side. It was Bill, the officer who had watched his star sight – the one who had been so delighted to inform him, confidentially, that the sea contained wonders.

'Are you hurt, lad?' he asked. 'What do you need?' – and, over his shoulder – 'Someone get blankets!'

Dylan shook his head. Bill gently touched his arm, which the sea had washed clean of silver; the hagflesh was now marbled like a bruise, his own flesh ghostly white around it. He looked at Dylan, eyes full of wordless question.

At their side, Captain Groves had hurried over to see to

Rose, and someone else was crouching by the twin. Small flecks of black were speckling Dylan's vision.

'That thing – it had all three of you?' said Bill – scrabbling to make sense of what he had just seen.

'Yes,' lied Dylan. This seemed safest.

Bill looked out to sea, where he believed a monster had just slipped back into a home fathoms deep. He seemed very far away, through the speckles of darkness. Dylan wondered what he would say if he knew that the monsters didn't live in the sea, but amongst men, in normal skin and bones. Somehow, the thought almost made him laugh.

A blanket appeared, and Dylan was swaddled like a baby. He had stopped paying attention by then; he was a little preoccupied with his heartbeat, which seemed slow and laboured, as though it was remembering how to function after a long absence. Arms were lifting him – he wasn't sure whose arms, or why . . .

. . . and the blackness was complete, and he slipped away inside it.

He was in a new cabin: there was something different about the light. A face was above him, with big blue eyes, and a tufty moustache.

'Aha!' said the face. 'You're awake. Excellent. My name's Marston – ship's medic. You're in the infirmary. Nasty scare you gave us, young man.'

Dylan considered this, blinked heavily, and slipped back into the black.

*

The next time he woke, there was no face above, but a little 'Oh!' at his side told him to turn his head – and there was Uncle Firth, squatting at the bedside.

'Welcome back, Dylan!' he said, beaming. 'Here, quick, drink this before the healer comes back' – he passed over a tin cup. 'He's almost entirely useless, I'm afraid.'

From long experience, Dylan downed the cup swiftly before he could register the taste and change his mind. It tasted how nettles felt, and made him shudder violently. He felt well, but very tired.

'I have to go,' he said. 'Mam and Dad . . .'

'Slow down,' said Uncle Firth, a hand on his shoulder. 'For now, the ship's still getting you closer to the Sargasso. I'm treating some samples of the silver in every way I can think of to see what will help. They're brewing. We'll try the silvers when they're ready.'

Dylan had little energy to protest. 'And the others . . . ?' he said, propping himself up on one elbow. He could see the twin in one bed against the opposite wall; at the far end, another contained a quilt full of an anonymous somebody.

'Both all right. Rose is having coughing fits, and mostly sleeping.'

'But she's all right? She'll live?'

'Yes, the healer seems confident,' said Uncle Firth. So the wreck-water had saved her. He went on, 'Captain Groves has been here – apparently she's his daughter . . .'

'Ah,' said Dylan. The captain's daughter . . . He remembered the captain talking to her at the rails, that first day, and crouching at her side on the deck as they were thrown back on board. She knew all about the speed of the ship, and had seen merfolk miles out in the Atlantic. He thought of the bright coverlet and pictures in her tin-can cabin – her home.

'So I take it,' said Uncle Firth delicately, 'that means she's not . . . ?'

'She's not the hag,' agreed Dylan. 'I saw them both down there at the same time.' He lay back down. The burst of energy involved in sitting had been over-ambitious. *She was alive.* He was, once again, not a murderer.

'Right,' said Uncle Firth. 'Well, that's it. I am going to kill that kelpie.'

'The kelpie's all right? And Caspian?'

'The kelpie's still mooning around in bed. Caspian's doing remarkably well – strong as a wyrm, that boy.'

'Good – good. And which twin is it?'

'Ah,' said Uncle Firth. 'I was hoping you'd know. She's in and out of consciousness, but she's not making much sense.'

'Oh,' said Dylan. Feeling anything about this seemed unmanageably complicated. It would be so much simpler, urged his body, just to sleep.

Uncle Firth leaned over the bed, and his face loomed into Dylan's vision. There was a purpling bruise, spreading from his nose into a blossoming black eye. For a moment Dylan wondered what had happened; then he remembered. 'Sorry about the fight,' he murmured.

His uncle smiled, and Dylan found himself smiling back. It all seemed so irrelevant now. 'I'll live,' said Uncle Firth. Then, with mock gravity, he quoted old silvermen text: 'The Sea Weard is dangerous, and must be feared."

'Hey. I'm *very* fearsome.'

'Tell me that when you can get out of bed without wobbling.'

Dylan was sure he had a very witty retort to this, but it had just slipped out of sight; and then Uncle Firth's face was lost in darkness, and he was falling, back into the quiet.

The next time he woke, he knew at once that he was well. There seemed to be an extra amount of verve in each heartbeat and breath, as though his own spirit was delighted to have reclaimed its rightful place in control of his body. Outside the porthole, the sky was blue.

Dylan pushed himself up, and looked over at the bed opposite. Uncle Firth was gone, but a sister sat awake, dressed in a landman nightgown, eating breakfast. She was pale and limp, sick from far too long in the wreck-water; but she half turned her head and smiled at him, the most familiar smile in the world. It was Tor's smile, when she had brought him a present from the village; it was Meriel's, when something had hatched in one of their tanks, and needed to be named. Why couldn't he tell?

Panic rose up in him like a wave. He didn't want to know. He wasn't ready to lose either of them.

'Good morning,' said the twin, 'smallest monster.'

20

It was uncanny, this sister who did not quite look like Meriel or like Tor. As Dylan met her gaze, he found himself strangely repulsed.

The wreck-water had slowed the twin's movements. It gave her a certain Meriel-like solemnity. 'Meriel?' Dylan tried, uncertainly.

The twin smiled, slow motion, lips spreading slowly outwards. 'Hello, ' she said.

'It *is* you? What happened to Tor? Is she all right?'

'Yes,' she said. 'I'm Tor too.'

'What?'

His sister turned her body to face him properly, slowly, rediscovering each muscle as she moved. Face-on, she looked more like a stranger than ever.

'I'm Meriel *and* I'm Tor,' she said. 'I'm both of us.'

'I don't . . .'

'The nál was feeding, and our human spirit was getting dangerously low, so we sort of – merged. It saved our lives.'

Dylan stared. This wasn't Lore he had heard of, and he didn't understand it. 'What? So who am I talking to right now?'

'Me. Both of us.'

'Right, but – who's controlling your mouth?' The question alone horrified Dylan. He knew what it was to share your body with another self, but his had to wait its turn. It couldn't jostle for his tongue or his hands or his feet.

His confusion seemed to be upsetting the twin; her face rearranged itself into anxiety in painful slow motion. 'It's not like that,' she said. 'I'm one person. Oh, it's so hard to describe . . . I can feel both people in me, but it's a bit like when part of you wants to stay outside and part of you wants to be home and warm. Or you're partly reading and partly knitting and partly listening to a bird outside. I'm just – both things at once.'

'So you're not hurt?' said Dylan. This felt like what he ought to say. What he wanted to say was: you can't be both at once, because then you're neither of my sisters, and I want them back; and *how* did this happen? But the wreck-water had left this new Tor-Meriel sister so weak and pale and stately-slow – more like a cloud than a person – and it felt as though if he panicked out loud then she might just gust apart.

Tor-Meriel turned her head left to right in one long, careful shake. 'I'm sick from the wreck-water. I'm not going to be able to help you – in the sea – I don't think. But merging hasn't hurt me. It's saved me.'

Dylan forced himself to say, 'Good. That's good,' and hold her gaze. But he couldn't think of a single thing more to say that wasn't cruel.

'I'm still me, Dylan,' she said, 'just *both* of me – can you understand that?' And when Dylan still couldn't find anything kind to say, she began, softly, to cry: slow, silent, rolling tears. Without thinking Dylan was out of bed and at her bedside, holding the familiar hand, which squeezed back feebly.

'Sorry,' she said. 'I mean it, I'm not hurt. But you're looking at me like you don't know me. And it's so strange – I'm used to having a twin. I've never been alone like this . . .'

'But you're both in there still?'

Somehow this was the wrong thing to say; she started to sob in earnest. 'Y-yes,' she said, 'but I m-miss there being another body – we were always together, we shared a bed, we shared everything . . . Being alone in the wreck was awful. You have to have someone outside your own head.'

This last part, at least, Dylan understood. He made himself lean forward and hug this sobbing sister, who didn't lean her head against his quite like Meriel or squeeze him quite like Tor, as he said, 'You've got me. I'm here.' And as she leaned into him, he repeated, 'I'm here. I'm here now. Hey – shh.'

When her breathing had slowed he eased himself away, fighting to keep his face neutral. The embrace had felt so familiar and so strange at once that it had ripped reality into two: this was his sister, and it was not his sister, at the same time.

'Thank you,' said Tor-Meriel, sinking back against the pillows. 'I – it's just so confusing.'

This was an understatement. 'I didn't even know it could happen,' said Dylan. 'How . . . ?'

'We're twins,' she said. 'We were already the same, underneath. Think of it like a sea sponge putting itself back together.'

'But there's nothing about that in the Lore,' said Dylan. 'How did you know what to do? Or did it just happen?'

Tor-Meriel considered this, chewing her lip like Tor. 'It's complicated,' she said at last. 'It's all part of a bigger thing . . . It's probably best if I tell you. Mam and Dad were going to tell you when you came of age. They only told us when *we* came of age.'

'What?' said Dylan, lost.

Tor-Meriel wiped her eyes. She seemed to be preparing herself for something, and it gave Dylan a queasy feeling. What could she have to tell him that was so hard to say?

'So, when I was two people,' she began, 'I was twins. I mean, obviously.'

'Yes,' said Dylan, 'I'm with you so far.'

'Right,' she said. 'Well, that's more normal, when you're born a wyrm. Having a twin. Mam and Dad were infected so it's different. But when you're born a wyrm, you get double the sea-spirit, and it's a lot for one body. Most of us sort-of split in the womb. That's why we can fuse again – the spirit is already one, underneath.' Now she was truly underway, Tor-Meriel seemed to be gathering strength. 'If there's affinity of spirit,' she explained, very Meriel-ish, 'you can share it by blood. The nál had left one of our heads a little loose – I was able to bite at my side, and my twin's, and share spirit through the wound. I didn't know quite how it would work – but as you can see . . .' She trailed away, then added, more to herself, 'The nál was away, and I think something hurt it – the currents that held us were weaker, for a moment – still, we nearly didn't get out . . .'

Dylan frowned. 'So wait,' he said, 'what weren't Mam and Dad telling me? That I'm unusual for not being a twin?'

'Exactly,' said Tor-Meriel. 'It means you got twice as much sea-spirit. Making you by far the strongest of us, smallest monster.'

'But why would they not tell me that?' said Dylan.

'They didn't want you to be discouraged. Knowing your sea-self was twice as strong . . . They really were going to tell you. They only told us first because they knew we were going to see all the other pairs, and wonder.'

Dylan had always known that the Lore said there were two in a Weard – but he had taken this as an instruction, not a description. 'How unusual is it then, to be like me?' said Dylan. 'Are there many others?' Maybe they could help him, teach him . . .

'There are legends—' said Tor-Meriel.

'*Legends?*'

'Yes – some of—'

'There's no one alive?'

Tor-Meriel seemed to sag slightly under his raised voice, but he couldn't help it; he couldn't keep his horror contained.

'No,' she said quietly.

'All right then, what do these *legends* say?' he demanded. He knew that this was not his sister's fault. But she was looking at him with a compassion that was not quite Meriel's quiet understanding or Tor's wide-open kindness, and it was awful.

'Well, one of them was really amazing,' she said earnestly. 'They fought off some of the sea's worst killers, and were responsible for a lot of the early bindings – náls and brimgasts and all sorts.'

'And the rest?'

She dropped her gaze. 'It's a lot of old landman stuff – you know, slaying the beast, all that nonsense. And some of them just lost their human side in the end, and lived at sea.' She looked up again, and added, 'Mam and Dad reckon you must be incredibly strong, not to have let that happen already.'

'Oh, good, well done me,' said Dylan. 'I can just stay and terrorise the land then. I assume that's why the landmen were busy slaying all the others? For killing innocent people?'

Tor-Meriel said nothing; only looked at him with that not-quite-right compassion.

'I can't *believe* they didn't tell me!' Although, even as he said it, Dylan knew this wasn't true. He could believe it easily. They wouldn't have wanted to accept what he was – they would have hoped that if they just willed it hard enough, they could make him something else. That was how it was, to love people deep in the root like they did. They *had* to love him; they had to believe he deserved it.

'Dylan,' said Tor-Meriel, 'please – don't let this stop you. You need to find a way to change back. The nál has all of us – not just Mam and Dad – everyone.'

Dylan did not reply. He put his head in his hands.

'It's so much stronger now – it's disrupting whole seas. We need someone like you, now –'

'You don't need to preach to me about it,' Dylan said, a little too loudly. 'I *know*. I've come all this way for you and

Mam and Dad and I'm obviously going to do whatever needs doing. I'll do anything I can to get my sea-self back. But I hate being what I am. I hate it!' He felt as though a bung had been pulled somewhere inside him, and he was filling up with everything he had never said, and sinking fast. 'Did Uncle Firth tell you,' he went on, words overflowing now, 'that I did it on purpose – the hag attack? And when it was done, before I saw that you were all in trouble, I was so happy. *So* happy. When it rained it felt like – like this soft tapping against my skin – it's so magical, you have no idea. I loved it. I don't want to be necessary. I want to be happy.'

'I thought you *were* happy,' said Tor-Meriel softly. 'I thought we all were.'

'That's not true,' said Dylan. 'Tor knew.' He wanted Tor then, badly.

'No,' said Tor-Meriel. 'I knew it was hard sometimes. But that's not the same thing.'

There was the click of a latch to their left just then, and the door opened. Dylan quickly stood, composing his face, and turned to see the ship's medic.

'Aha!' said Marston, beaming. 'Two patients awake! Excellent.' And he looked from one to the other, apparently not seeing anything to contradict this assessment. 'And how are we feeling?'

'Fine,' said Dylan and Tor-Meriel in ludicrous sing-song unison.

'Splendid. I'm going to bring you both some lunch. We'll see if you've got your appetites back.' He looked over to Rose's bed. 'Sleeping again, I see. Well, I'll bring a third portion just in case.' And he ducked back into the corridor, delighted by the progress of his wards, and the prospect of lunch.

When he had gone, there was a short silence.

'Maybe I shouldn't have told you,' said Tor-Meriel.

'What difference would it make?' said Dylan. 'I am what I am.'

'You'll still change back? If Uncle Firth can work out the silver?'

'Of course,' said Dylan.

There was no other choice.

Tor-Meriel slept again soon after that. Dylan could not, although when Uncle Firth came in, he pretended. He felt as though he would never sleep again: every nerve was wide awake.

As the hours wore on, the portholes clouded and the light in the cabin grew dim, and a storm began. Dylan knew this because the ship began to seesaw wildly, and he made the unwelcome discovery that on this side of the waves, he was capable of full-blown seasickness. He shut his eyes against the rocking motion, but it didn't help.

He was so lost in his own thoughts that when he opened his eyes to find Rose kneeling at his bedside, it startled him.

'Oh! You're up!' he said – a little stupidly. Apparently, knowing that she was not in fact eating his spirit did not make him any less stupid around her. It didn't help that he was trying not to remember yelling at her about being alluring; the urge to hit his head hard against something was back, with a vengeance.

She opened her mouth as though to say something, but seemed lost.

'I owe you an apology,' said Dylan, holding on to his one clear thought. 'We thought you were – er, there's this creature following me, and we thought it might be a shapeshifter, like me. So I thought you might be the hag – that's what it's called. We were given this sort-of prophecy, and I thought you were here alone, but now my uncle says the captain is your father . . .' He was not at all sure this was clear; he tried to come to the point. 'Anyway, that's why I was so rude. I'm really sorry.'

She made a noise then, but it was more like a half-sob than speech. He leaned forward a little, instinctually. The ship lurched queasily.

'I'll tell you all about us,' he said impulsively. 'It's the least I can do. I'd like to.'

And then she leaned in towards him, and the almost-dizzy feeling was between them again, and without thinking Dylan leaned closer –

– and she opened her mouth, and between her lips bright red flesh forced itself out like a tentacle. The hag's body had become one long thin rope, which now bulged and rearranged itself under its skin as it burst into freedom. It was over before Dylan could do more than yell: in seconds the whole hag had blossomed from her mouth.

It must have stowed away inside her unconscious, drowning body. He had barely comprehended this when she fell back, discarded, and the hag lunged for his throat.

21

This time there was nowhere to escape to. Dylan's yell of shock was cut short by needle teeth puncturing his windpipe. His next breath burned him, and he choked. The hag clung on, winding itself over his right shoulder; then the bite tightened, and so did the flesh at his wrists and rib, and all three were feeding at once.

He wasn't sure how much time he had before his sea-self was killed. It didn't feel like it could be long.

Dimly, he was aware that Tor-Meriel was screaming. She seemed very far away. Dylan was somewhere deep inside his own body now, fighting for control. With a wrench, he forced himself out of the bed.

He didn't know how to use the sea-silver, but it was the only hope he could think of. He staggered to the door, and out into the corridor. Leaning against the wall, he made his way to the bathroom and the kobold.

This was a dizzying effort. When he arrived he was burning hot, and everything seemed to be listing slightly, and in the far-away world outside his own body Caspian was blurring strangely, his shape dancing in and out of sense like a candle flame.

'Dylan!' Caspian was saying, all far-away urgency. 'How . . . ?'

Dylan was concentrating on picking up the kobold. This seemed almost impossible: he kept thinking he was bending himself, only to find it was the world that was bending. He managed it at last.

He had no idea what to do with the silver, and could only think of one person to ask. Clutching the half-full kobold, he threw himself bodily at the bathroom door, fell out into the corridor beyond, and crawled the unfathomable distance to his own cabin. The wrist with the flesh embedded was no longer any use, so with the other hand he scrabbled at the door handle. At last he was inside.

'Kelpie,' he croaked.

The kelpie was in bed with its back to him; it turned, and their eyes met. The hurricane-dark was much deeper than before, and Dylan understood then that it, too, was somewhere far inside itself.

Dylan held the kobold out. 'What do I do?'

For a moment he thought the kelpie wasn't going to answer. Then it dissolved into wind – and the room smelled of sweet, sad days at the end of autumn, in the last of the sun – and reappeared at Dylan's side. It cupped the kobold in both hands, and pushed it upwards, towards his chin. Ludicrously, the gesture felt like their farewell toast, and made Dylan want to say, 'May the sea keep your spirit in blood . . .'

But perhaps this was not ludicrous. In old Lore, the drink had included sea-silver. Mam and Dad had written off this instruction as superstition.

'Drink?' said Dylan.

The kelpie nodded, and tilted the kobold. Dylan's lips met lip-like kobold flesh. Messily, he drank.

The kelpie pulled away after his first gulp, holding up a hand: *enough*. For a moment, nothing changed.

Then the hag at his throat convulsed, tugging at Dylan with its teeth as it writhed, bringing him to the floor.

It took a few minutes, or perhaps an eternity, for the silver to reach all three pieces of the hag. The living creature at his throat fell first, unable to hang on for more than a few tainted breaths; it lay at his side, wheezing horribly. The piece at his wrist fought harder, bucking and squirming with every pulse of his heart; but as the silvered blood slowly poisoned it, the grip grew weaker, until Dylan hardly noticed when it finally fell away. By then, it was his ribs that seemed like they might crack open.

But the poison weakened that piece too, and his ribs survived; and when the last piece of hagflesh fell away, he was still alive. As he lay on his back in the dim cabin, the pulsing of the three wounds grew quieter, and the world was the right way up again, and Dylan realised – like somebody completing a simple sum – that he was going to live.

He held up his wrist, and looked at it. There were two small pinprick wounds, barely visible. Nearby, the breath of the hag was a despairing rattle. He closed his eyes.

*

He was still there when Uncle Firth found him.

'Dylan! Dylan?'

Dylan opened his eyes. 'Mmfine,' he said.

'What in the River . . . ?'

'The hag got in Rose,' Dylan mumbled. 'It got inside her, when we were in the sea. Hiding from the wreck-water, maybe . . . That's why the kelpie saw an attack . . .'

Uncle Firth was looking at something just out of Dylan's line of vision, his face full of wonder. 'It's dead,' he said.

But Dylan had already known this, without needing to look. He knew because outside, it was raining; and something inside him stirred at the call, and it was rattling his bones, and he ached from the inside out.

22

It was done, and now that he was himself, a puny ship was unnecessary. It was time to go to sea.

He pushed himself upright, very slowly. His muscles seemed to have been replaced with trembling threads.

Uncle Firth watched him, then said, 'Lie still. I'll go and make sweet flag tonic. And tell the others you're all right.'

'I've got to go.'

'It will take two minutes to drink a tonic. You're shaking.'

There was sense in this. Dylan watched his uncle leave the room without argument. For a few moments he sat silently, until the shaking was a little less violent. Then he pushed himself up to see the kelpie.

'Thank you,' he said, 'for trying to warn me. The hag *did* attack. It got inside her in the sea.'

The kelpie didn't respond, and the darkness in its eyes seemed deeper than ever.

'Sea-silver poisons spirit-eaters, if I drink it,' said Dylan. 'Have I understood that right? Would it work on the nál?'

The kelpie nodded once, gravely, and the sad-autumn smell intensified.

Dylan squatted shakily at its side, and asked, 'Are you dying?'

'Fog,' replied the kelpie.

'What can we get you?'

The kelpie looked at him mutely, with a louder silence than usual, as though there was something in particular it was not saying. Dylan had the feeling he so often had, talking to anyone outside his own family – that some rules were at play that no one had told him about. 'Anything at all?' he said. 'Is there some way we can help?'

But the kelpie still didn't reply. Uncle Firth returned with the tonic, and Dylan followed him back to the other cabin, not wanting to stay alone with the shivering spirit. Inside, he found his uncanny sister talking to Rose.

The image of Rose falling back, discarded, was still vivid in his mind; it was jarring to find her conscious and upright, sitting on her bed, listening to Tor-Meriel with rapt attention.

'Dylan!' she said when he came in. 'You're a *water-dragon*?'

Dylan looked at the twin, who shrugged apologetically. Water-dragon was one of their least favourite names, but it was one that modern landmen knew, and it was better than loch monster. 'I don't breathe fire though,' he said. 'Sorry. Are you all right?'

Rose spread her hands, as though to say, *I seem to be*. 'It was horrible,' she said. 'Like feeling sick but not being sick, and suffocating at the same time. But now I feel really light. Like the good feeling after being ill.' She stretched. 'I'm all achey on the inside though. I can feel every corner of my intestines.'

Uncle Firth wrinkled his nose as he handed Dylan the tonic, saying, 'Drink up. Small sips, it's strong stuff – careful.'

Dylan found his hands were still shaking enough to make it hard to hold the brew still. He needed it badly. He took a sip, and shuddered. On her bed, Rose began coughing – a wheezing, broken sound.

'I'm sorry,' said Dylan, when she had subsided. 'You shouldn't have been caught up in any of this.'

'Why are you sorry? *I* followed you.'

'Yes, but . . .' Dylan didn't know where to begin.

'But what?'

'But you're a landman,' said Dylan. 'We're not meant to let you get caught up in this kind of thing.'

'Whose rule is that? Is there some kind of dragon council of Great Britain?'

'No – it's just us . . .'

'So who says?'

The sweet-flag was already doing Dylan good, but still, he found himself flailing weakly under this onslaught. His waking sea-self wasn't helping. 'It's just – sea stuff is dangerous.'

'Also,' added Tor-Meriel, 'landmen do have a tendency to try and kill us.'

Rose drew her knees up to her chin, with her moon face perched on top. 'I don't care about dangerous!' she said. 'I had that thing inside me and I still don't care. You have no idea how lonely and dreary I'd been feeling, stuck on this ship, and then I met you, and a *merman*, and there's a whole other world . . . I don't want to be left on the outside of it all.'

Dylan looked at her, sitting on a soft quilt in a white cotton gown, all calm determination while the rain battered the window, and he wanted to tell her that she was already on the inside. That *was* the inside – sharing the quiet, steady earth with your own kind. But he didn't have the words, and anyway this was a useless argument, and there was no time. So he just said, truthfully, 'Well – I'm just glad you're all right.'

'And I'm glad *you're* all right,' said Rose. 'What is it he has to go and fight now?' She addressed this to Tor-Meriel, whom she had clearly found to be a more reliable source of straightforward explanations.

'A spirit-eater,' said Tor-Meriel. 'We call it a nál. You might know it as the Bermuda Triangle – it draws in prey.'

'The Bermuda Triangle is real?' said Rose. 'And mermaids . . . How many of our stories are real?'

'Oh, some. We don't know all the answers either, honestly, there's so much we don't know. The Sargasso's especially weird. Every European eel is born there and goes back there to die and we don't know why – isn't that bizarre?' And the way her eyes lit up for this fact was so Meriel-like that Dylan suddenly felt tears starting in his eyes, and he had to look away from his mixed-up sister for a moment. He looked at Uncle Firth instead, and he knew they were both remembering Meriel in the front room, a lifetime ago.

'The Bermuda Triangle thing happens when it's only just started to get loose,' she went on, oblivious. 'So you can imagine an unbound nál is very bad.'

'Did you say the nál was away, when you left?' said Dylan. 'And you thought it had been hurt?'

'Yes – although I'm just guessing about the second part,' said Tor-Meriel. 'All its currents just fell slack for a moment, like it had slipped. And they sort of spasmed a bit.'

Dylan thought of the peeled-off pieces of hag writhing in pain under his skin whenever the hag was hurt. 'Right. Sounds likely. Well, let's hope it's still hurt – or still away – or both. When did you leave?'

'I'm not sure exactly – yesterday morning, maybe?'

'How do you hurt a current?' asked Rose.

'You can't,' said Dylan. 'That's why we have to bind it. It would have been hurt in its other shape – it's a serpent – like a bigger version of us.'

'It's got other shapes too,' said Tor-Meriel.

'What?' Dylan asked, surprised – and then surprised at himself for being surprised. Would he ever learn not to assume he knew the sea? 'What are they? Do I need to know about them?'

'I think it can look like almost anything it's consumed,' said Tor-Meriel. 'Every time it coils round it changes again. But I'm sure it will be current or serpent to fight you. The others are smaller.' She considered, as though sorting through confused memories. 'There's a lot of variations on squid, and one thing that I think might be a very ancient kind of shark. Sometimes it's a golden water horse. One time it came round to inspect us all, and it was just a boy, I saw him very clearly – merfolk, quite beautiful, exactly half-and-half like a picture of a mermaid.'

Uncle Firth let out a little 'Oh!' of surprise, and looked sharply at Dylan.

Dylan looked back, nonplussed. 'What?'

'Well – maybe not – but – Caspian was injured yesterday morning, Dylan. That's around when something hurt the nál.'

Dylan laughed. 'Really? You didn't believe Rose was the hag, but you think Caspian might be a nál?' And when Uncle Firth looked uncertain, he said, 'He's been helping me.'

'Well – yes. Helping you get closer to the Sargasso . . . He *is* infected very neatly from the waist down, that's quite unusual . . .'

'Who's Caspian?' said Tor-Meriel.

'A merfolk boy,' said Dylan. 'He helped me back at home, after you went missing. He saved me at the Ridge. And it was him who told me you were in the *Titanic*.'

That made Tor-Meriel frown. 'How did he know that?' she said.

'I don't know,' said Dylan, feeling defensive now. 'Folk know things. They knew about the nál.'

'Yes, but that's a *nál*. The whole point is it distorts whole oceans. I'm just a little wyrm.'

'Well . . .'

'And if he was at home when you left, how did he get out to the Ridge so fast?'

Dylan opened his mouth to reply, then realised he didn't have an answer, and shut it. Grandpa had said a message was being sent by merlight to the folk already out in open ocean. Dylan hadn't stopped to calculate whether Caspian had had time to join them.

'Oh, River . . .' said Uncle Firth. He was clearly thinking along similar lines.

'I'm sure that can be explained,' said Dylan. And when none of the others agreed, or offered an explanation, he said, 'Come *on*. This is silly.'

'Should we go and investigate it at least?' said Rose. 'Ask him some questions before you go? If it is him we can just – knock him out, or something.'

'He isn't –' Dylan began to protest. But everyone else was getting to their feet – even, shakily, Tor-Meriel – so he downed the last of his tonic and followed them to the door, protesting as they went; a rag-tag parade with Rose leading the charge, off to interrogate an injured boy with her rock-like determination about something she couldn't possibly begin to understand.

'This is stupid,' said Dylan, a little too loudly. There was a heavy weight in his stomach. No one answered him.

Rose pushed open the door.

Inside, the bathtub had cracked in two. On the floor, water and sea-silver lay pooled and sparkling in the light that fell through the smashed porthole.

Caspian was gone.

23

'I don't understand,' said Dylan, staring. 'He was helping me.'

'He helped get two missing wyrms to the Sargasso Sea, within his reach,' said Uncle Firth gently. 'I don't know exactly how a nál thinks, but I imagine he had his reasons.'

'But,' said Dylan – his brain seemed to be stuck – 'he was a friend.'

Nobody else seemed particularly concerned by this. Uncle Firth and Tor-Meriel were eagerly swapping descriptions and deductions, while Rose listened, rapt. Yes, the merfolk man Tor-Meriel had seen matched the description of Caspian. Yes, he had been healing freakishly fast. They were agreeing with each other in eager excitement.

Dylan could only think, stupidly, of all the things Caspian had said that would have to be lies if this was true. He had never made a friend before, or lost one. He was entirely new to the lurching feeling when you realise you have misjudged someone; like missing a step, and tumbling down unexpectedly.

'Why didn't he just feed on me back in the firth, then?' he said – as though he could logically reason away the blinding evidence of the empty, broken room. And there was the way

Caspian's shape had seemed to be flickering and changing, the last time they had seen each other. Dylan had put it down to his own feverish state.

'Different selves are tied to different places, right?' said Rose. 'Your sister was saying. Can he be the current-thingy outside the Sargasso?'

Dylan looked at Tor-Meriel, who shrugged. They didn't know. 'I suppose not,' said the twin. 'That would fit the evidence.'

'If he's been weak all this time,' said Uncle Firth, 'then should we expect a stronger pull on the ship now he's restored?'

More things they didn't know. Not-knowing was exhausting. Numbly, Dylan pulled himself back to the task at hand.

'I'll get the bandoleer and go,' he said.

'Wait – I'll come –' said Uncle Firth; and Tor-Meriel followed with a slow but determined shuffle; and Rose strode off at speed, keeping one step ahead of Dylan. The others all occupied each other with general hubbub in the corridor while Dylan prepared. He checked all the weapons in the bandoleer; he checked the still-swirling vials of his parents' blood, then took out his own vial, went to the bathroom, and emptied it; he used the vial to take a little fresh sea-silver from the kobold. It occurred to him, too late, that if anything happened to him the others would now have no blood to see if he was alive. He didn't dwell on that. He stowed the vial in the bandoleer too, then went to squat at the kelpie's bedside. It stared up at him.

'Caspian was the nál,' said Dylan.

The kelpie did not reply.

'Well,' said Dylan, 'I'm going.'

'Dylan Pade,' said the kelpie. With an enormous effort, it gusted itself out of bed, and over to the door. The sad autumn smell was gone; the kelpie now smelled faintly of decay.

Dylan followed, went out into the corridor, and pushed through the others towards the door.

They strode and shuffled and gusted behind and beside him, but Dylan felt far away from them. He was going through the motions of the plan, but it seemed unreal. He had always been prepared to fight. He would have been ready to kill, if he could, the faceless force that held his family – tear it apart – stamp it out without a second thought, just as you would stamp out a meaningless spark that is threatening to set the world on fire.

He had not prepared himself for fighting Caspian.

It was only once they were on deck that they realised something was very wrong with the ship.

Around them, the storm continued to pull the waves, but the ship no longer rose and fell. Instead something stronger than the storm was dragging it side-on through the waves, carving out a flattened and frothing wake, moving at a terrifying speed. The disturbed water roared. Through the sound, small and reedy, Dylan could hear the gaggle of raised voices from the fo'c'sle: looking back he could see all of the ships' officers there, gathered in panic.

'He's pulling us in?' Dylan addressed this to Tor-Meriel, shouting to be heard over the water. They had known this nál to sink ships directly overhead, but the *Rose Marie* was still far north of the Sargasso. Restored to his full strength, Caspian was incredible.

'The stories said it was strong, unbound,' the twin yelled, 'but I had no idea . . .'

Dylan was trying to think of something practical, but all he could think was that Caspian had made sure Tor-Meriel would be on the ship that he was now reeling in. The last wyrm had been rooted out from its hiding place.

'Might the sea-silver nets work as a ward?' asked Uncle Firth. He kept his voice calm, but he was gripping the railings so hard his knuckles were white, staring out at the churning salt water.

Dylan shook his head. 'We might have enough to protect a small boat,' he said. 'Not a ship this size.'

'Could you help?' said Rose to the kelpie. 'You're a wind spirit, right?'

The kelpie spread its hands. Dylan could see right through it to the deck behind. It was clear to everyone that it was much too weak; it seemed surprising, when you looked closely, that it was standing upright at all. There was a moment's silence on the deck, while wind wailed and waves crashed and the displaced ocean rumbled like a waterfall beneath the ship.

'Dylan,' called Uncle Firth, 'do you have a knife in that bandoleer?'

Dylan took the knife from its sheath and passed it over without question. He had been in enough danger with his family to know that you did what you were asked, immediately.

But as Uncle Firth took the knife, and Dylan saw his eyes were fixed on the kelpie with hatred, he faltered. 'Wait,' he said, 'what are you going to do?'

By way of an answer, Uncle Firth ran the knife in one swift movement across the top of his own forearm. Red blood welled up. He thrust the arm at the kelpie.

'This is what you need, isn't it?'

The kelpie pressed both hands to its chest, and bowed its head. 'Firth Pade,' it said.

'Shut up,' replied Uncle Firth. 'Drink.'

The Weard were no stranger to blood or to spirits, but both Dylan and Tor-Meriel had to quickly look away when the kelpie drank. Dylan would have been hard-pressed to say what was so repulsive. It wasn't really the red blood, or the lapping tongue of the man-formed kelpie. It was more the look in Uncle Firth's eyes as the blood was taken from him – as he became, for one long minute, prey.

When they finished and Dylan looked back again, Uncle Firth was pale, and he curled himself down into a crouch now to keep from fainting. But the kelpie was solid again, and significantly taller than a normal man. Dylan had to crane up to look in its eyes. When he did, they dragged at him like night devouring day.

Then it was unspooling into wind, with a howl that echoed out across the churning wake and the waves beyond. All of them staggered as the wind spirit rushed over the ship, and Tor-Meriel fell to the deck. Against the side of the ship, the kelpie began to blow in earnest.

For a moment, the *Rose Marie* rocked wildly, and its stern

swung in semi-circles of confusion. Gradually, the rocking and spinning stopped. Then it began to slow, and the roar of the water below it was soothed.

The kelpie howled, and the ship was brought to a restful drift. It didn't quite stop. But it was slow enough to buy them time.

'How long can it keep going?' yelled Rose.

They looked at each other. No one knew.

'Well,' said Dylan. 'Better get going, then.'

The howl from the kelpie intensified. It sounded like wind, but also like a war cry.

'Dylan,' said Uncle Firth urgently, looking up from his crouch, 'just try and get the others out, that's still your priority. Don't fight it unless you have to . . .'

Dylan did not reply. Rescuing the other wyrms *was* the priority, and he would do that first. But now, if he didn't also try and fight this thing – at least weaken it, even if he couldn't bind it – it was going to sink the ship. Uncle Firth knew that, but he was being Uncle-Firth-ish and noble about it. Well, they were both capable of being stupid and noble.

'Where will the wyrms go once you free them?' said Tor-Meriel. 'They could barely fight this pull at full strength, and they'll be half-dead.'

This froze Dylan, hand at his shirt buttons. The Sargasso was true open ocean, miles from the nearest shore. The pull of the nál would be significantly stronger below the surface. He doubted he could carry even one adult wyrm against this flow to the land.

'If they could make it to the ship . . . ?' he said.

Tor-Meriel shook her head. 'We're miles away. And if we were close enough, we'd be sinking.'

'If we had a smaller boat we could take over there,' said Dylan, 'then the silver nets might be able to go all the way around it, enough for a ward . . .'

'The lifeboat,' said Rose.

The weardkin of the British Isles looked at her, nonplussed. With her curls whirling in the wind, standing resolute in the falling rain, she had never looked more like she belonged to the sea.

'The what-boat?' yelled Tor-Meriel.

'There's a rowboat here – in case the ship sinks. We could use that.'

'We'd need someone on board it to work the nets,' shouted Dylan.

'I'll come,' said Rose immediately.

'No – you don't have to. Someone who—'

'Dylan!' Rose had started setting off down the deck, but she turned back now, hands on hips. 'If we don't do anything, we're all going to die. Your sister can barely stand. Your uncle will shrivel up and die if he falls in sea water. I'm here now whether you like it or not, and I'm not sick or amphibious or secretly a sea-spirit, so stop being so bloody chivalrous and let me help!'

And without waiting for an answer, she stamped off down the deck. The others all looked at each other. Then, for want of a better plan, they followed in her wake.

She led them to the rowboat at the aft, which was protected by a thick cream rainproof cover. She began unfastening the cover, and the others joined her, then copied her as she took the ropes coiled inside and laid them out on the deck. The rain intensified as they worked, soaking Dylan's shirt and making his whole skin vibrate.

The boat had oars inside, and benches to seat maybe thirty people squeezed together. It was attached by ropes to two cranks, flanking it on either side. 'Swing it out,' yelled Rose, positioning herself at one of the cranks, and pointing to the other. Dylan scrambled to obey, and they turned the heavy cranks until the boat hovered out over the sea, parallel with the deck.

Rose looked at Uncle Firth and Tor-Meriel: one nursing a bloodied arm, the other sea-foam-white and leaning against the rail for support. 'We need you to lower us,' she said. 'Can you do it?'

They both straightened up, and nodded.

Dylan and Rose clambered into the boat, and Tor-Meriel handed the bandoleer after them. Then she grabbed at Dylan's hand, eyes wide with panic. Dylan understood. Now it was his sister, not him, who might have to return to the gingerbread cottage alone. In that moment, his ambivalence to this strange new sister slipped away: she was all he had of Meriel and of Tor, and he loved her.

'Be careful!' she called uselessly. And at the same time Uncle Firth hollered, 'Ready?'

Dylan thought his sister said something else, but it was lost in the storm. Then her face withdrew, and they began to lower the boat.

They were not skilled at the job, and even with Uncle

Firth's injured arm, Tor-Meriel was much weaker than him. In the end he mostly ran between both winches. The boat see-sawed horribly – now lowering the stern, now the bow. Dylan and Rose gripped the sides, and kept stoic eyes on the bottom of the boat. Dylan was thankful that the *Rose Marie* no longer rocked on the storm; they would surely have been smashed to pieces against her side, dangling from their precarious ropes.

They had barely begun their descent when the faces of deckhands appeared – and Captain Groves. Dark curling beard gaped down at dark curling head.

'Rosie,' he yelled. 'What are you *doing*? Get back here!'

Rose looked up at him. 'We're going to stop what's happening,' she called. From her dismissive tone, it was clear that she was not in the habit of involving her father in her decisions.

The captain protested, but his words were half lost under the waves. Something he said made another deckhand put a threatening arm on Uncle Firth's shoulder. But beside him, Bill leaned forward. 'You know something about this?' he bellowed to Dylan.

'Yes!' Dylan called back.

'Are we going to die?'

The boat lurched down on Rose's side as Firth managed another turn of the winch, and both of them swayed. Dylan caught himself, then shouted, 'I don't know. I'm trying to stop it.'

Bill nodded, and for a few long moments he stared at Dylan, as though he had already transformed before his eyes. Then he turned and set to work at the other winch. There was a tussle overhead, but Dylan didn't see who was on whose side; he only knew that there was shouting, and the little boat hurried like a rocking horse down the side of the ship, and his stomach joined the motion.

At last the boat was patted gently on to the skin of the sea, as though afraid to disturb it, before landing properly in the water.

Bill leaned over the rails, and at the top of his lungs, he called, 'Who are you?'

'The Sea Weard of the British Isles,' Dylan replied. But he didn't know if anyone had heard him. He and Rose looked at each other, and Dylan found himself grinning with a sort of hysterical relief.

'Well,' he said, 'I wasn't expecting *that* to be the worst part.'

'We should get some sort of bravery medal for that alone,' agreed Rose. She looked up once more, at her father and the others. To Dylan they already felt very far away.

The moment they were free of the *Rose Marie*, the wind of the kelpie let up, just long enough for an in-breath – just long enough to release them. The little boat whirled away on the nál's drag like a feather. Before the heavy *Rose Marie* could do more than lurch forwards, the kelpie resumed its push.

Dylan waved at the sky, and called, 'Thank you!' But the steady howl was the only reply.

'Ready?' he said to Rose – as though there was any choice, now that they were skimming across the open sea.

She sat alert in the little boat, every muscle ready to spring, eyes open wide enough to drink in the whole world.

'Ready,' she replied.

24

They sailed over the flattened and frothing grey Atlantic: it felt like riding over thunder clouds. Rose sat very straight, waiting for a signal. Dylan gave up looking for the signs of the great currents circling the Sargasso, or any other means of navigation in this strange sea. He just hoped it would be obvious when they were close.

It *was* obvious.

The grey sea began to lighten, and grow less opaque; Dylan realised he could see the shadows of fish through the waves. Spread out ahead of them, the lightness grew, reaching an intense shade of gold on the horizon – as though the sun was setting, but underneath the water, sending light upwards to the world above. There was no more rain here.

'Right,' said Dylan, with much more confidence than he felt. He took a silver net from his bandoleer, taken from Tor-Meriel's supplies, and a small knife. 'Could you hold this in place?' he said – and as Rose held the net against the outside edge of the boat, Dylan unfurled it until it ran around them on all sides. Where the two ends met, he nudged Rose's hand aside, and tacked it in place with the knife. Then he took the thread of the signal knots and tied it to the net, so it trailed into the water, extending far below.

'Signal knots,' he explained. 'The other wyrms know it. It's a sort of universal sign. They'll be able to feel the ripples it makes in the water over long distances.'

As he worked, the little boat had been slowing. For a minute now they waited, breath held. Gradually, it brought itself to a stop.

Dylan handed Rose a second smaller net. 'The main ward round the boat is to keep you from the overall drag,' he said. When he spoke about the practical matters of the Weard, he was a different sort of person, filled with a quiet confidence; she looked at him with curious surprise. 'You'll need to keep an eye on the knots – re-tie anything that gives – you should have a while before that starts happening. And if it comes at you with a tendril of water – kind of fishing for you – you'll want to use *this* net to try and catch it. Just skim it wherever you feel a pull. It's pretty powerful stuff. And the nál's power weakens abruptly at the surface, so it can be resisted, up here – very different below the surface. Do you want to try using it against the main drag, see what it feels like?'

So Rose took the net, and dropped it against the direction of the drag that hurried all around them, but no longer moved them. She stared. 'Huh,' she said. 'It's like catching the wind.'

'Yes!' said Dylan. 'I'd bring it back in for now. The knots weaken with use.'

'Right-o,' said Rose, hauling in the net. She folded it carefully, and draped it across her knees as she sat back down, all the time staring at the sea around them.

'What *is* this place?' she asked.

'The Sargasso Sea,' said Dylan. But he knew that didn't really answer the question. That was *where*, not *what*. For the enchantment around them, Dylan had no good explanation.

The sea was transparent and golden, glimmering on all sides of the boat like a vast pool of candlelight. They could see all the way to the seamounts to the north, and right down to the plains below; to the south, the view grew too blinding to make out clearly. That must be where the nál – Caspian – waited.

And towards this light, in a fantastical and helpless parade, the creatures of the sea were being pulled.

The larger creatures twisted and fought, while the smaller travelled limp and belly-up, mouths open in astonishment. Boarfish and redfish and small-eyed rabbitfish, sersids and blacksmelts and basslets; below them, the catshark and lanternshark, and the billowing bodies of rays; then the alien fish dragged up from the deep, skeletal and hideous in the bare light – viperfish and bristlemouths, dragonfish and seadevils and gaping black swallowers. Here and there, sperm whales and fin whales were dragged among them all like great stones.

In the distance, Dylan spotted two landman ships in the throng, noses pointed downwards in an unwilling dive. He looked over his shoulder to the northern horizon: no sign of the *Rose Marie*. Around their own little boat the nets were holding fast, and it was still, bobbing slightly as water and silver fought each other.

'Right,' said Dylan. 'Hopefully you'll start seeing the others soon. They'll come out of the water as wyrms, so you'll have to hold your nerve, but I promise they'll turn human by the time they hit the deck. Once you haven't seen anyone new for a few hours, turn back. And if the silver ward starts to weaken, turn back regardless. Get them back to the ship and Uncle Firth can tend to any injuries. You don't need to wait for me – I can swim faster than the ship now, I'll take care of myself.'

She nodded.

He sat quiet a moment, mentally making sure he had said everything he needed to say. Then he took the vial full of sea-silver from his bandoleer. He raised it to Rose. 'May the Sea keep your spirit in blood,' he said.

'What are you doing?' she said.

'A precaution.' Dylan took a sip of the silver, gagged, then made himself raise it again. A nál was much bigger than a hag. And he was about to be much bigger too: he could handle a little more silver. 'May the Sea keep your spirit in bone,' he said, and gulped a second time.

Once more for luck. His tongue felt thick with it. 'May the Sea keep your spirit in breath,' he said, and downed the last.

Rose watched him, frowning. 'What have you just done?' she said. And when he didn't immediately reply, she leaned forward, and said, 'You owe me. I'm part of this now. No more secrets; it isn't fair.'

Dylan nodded. 'It's poison,' he said, 'for spirit-eaters. If the nál eats me, it will die – hopefully – or it will weaken it at least, enough to free everything it's holding.'

She considered this. 'You're still leaving things out. What does it mean, if it eats you? Will you die?'

'I might,' Dylan said. 'Or it might be that only my sea-self lives. It'll eat my dormant spirit – my human-self – first.' He had not wanted to think about this. It was unreal to him, as dreamlike as the golden sea, but it was true: if he let himself be eaten, it was his human self that almost certainly wouldn't come back.

'You mean you'd stay in the sea?' said Rose.

'Yes.'

'And would that be – would you still be you, on the inside? Are you happy in the sea?'

'I don't really remember it. I think I'm happy there.'

'*Dylan*,' said Rose. She sounded exasperated.

'What?'

'Stop making me drag everything out of you. I can feel all the things you don't say, hovering around the edges all the time. You're happy there *but* . . . But what?'

Dylan knew she was right, but it was an old habit. He had had years of practice at not saying the parts of the story that didn't fit – the parts that turned Mam's eyes soft with worry, and made Dad too jolly, and set Tor off fussing and mothering. 'I hate my other shape,' he said. 'I'm so big and – alien – I love being human. I want to care about people, and have a home, and . . .' He gestured at the sea spreading all below them. 'The freedom down there is incredible. Sometimes I need the freedom so badly it feels like it will rip me apart. But I never really *want* to go to sea. I know as soon as I do, I won't care about anyone – I'll be alone.' He thought of Tor-Meriel, and the horror in her eyes as she had started crying: you have to have someone outside your own head.

He looked at Rose, and the giddiness was there again; and

she leaned in then, and kissed him. For half a moment, it felt strange. He had assumed he would feel something in his lips, since lips seemed to be the point. But instead he found the feeling was everywhere, and it was the feeling that she was close, so close that they blurred, and all his dread and horror was on the outside – like rain on the roof, while you stayed inside, warm and small and safe.

When they started to move apart, he shuffled himself closer and pulled her in again. He didn't want to stop, and step back outside.

But they had to, of course. The next time they pulled apart, he didn't resist.

'Just in case you don't come back,' said Rose, trying to make it sound jocular.

'Yes. Practical.'

'Well it seemed only fair. Since I've been temptressing you all this time with my great allure.'

'Oh, shut up.' And this time *he* was the one who kissed *her*, but it was shorter, and more like punctuation – like an exclamation mark, maybe – both of their mouths smiling as they met. He hadn't known there could be different kinds of kisses, that meant different things. He hadn't had time to find out.

And there wasn't time now: he had to go. If he put it off much longer, he wasn't sure he would be able to make himself do it.

'Right,' he said.

'Right,' she agreed.

He stood, turned his back to her and undressed quickly,

then shouldered the loops of the bandoleer. The cold Atlantic air bit his human skin, and every small hair stood on end. The silver made his blood beat loudly in his ears, a steady pulse, marching inside him, keeping him alive.

He hugged his arms around his ribs. He had loved, so much, being human.

He didn't turn around to say goodbye. What could he say? He leaned forward, and the rattle in his bones became a roar; and he slid under the surface, into the gold Sargasso Sea.

25

He unfurled like a dawn.
 Or rather, the world unfurled. Human skin is blind: it only sees what it touches. Like fish, a wyrm's skin can detect movement in the water all around them. Dylan's senses flowed outwards, and his mind filled with the fluttering of the struggling sea creatures, and the swirling of the surface water, and the bobbing of a small boat above, with the tattoo of water bending around the signal knot; and above all, with the intricate whorls of Caspian's design.

Because, of course, the currents he had set in motion *were* a design. Their echoes across the sea would be random chaos. But here, he had built a citadel.

Dylan resisted the great drag a moment, helped by the silver he carried, the bandoleer now stretched out into a single loop. He hung suspended, feeling the other currents of water the nál had made from itself. They crackled with golden light like a bright electrical charge, lighting up the sea around them. Long tentacles of current reached for food; by far the largest now was concentrated on the SS *Rose Marie*. The centre was protected by currents piled into great walls – or perhaps it was better to call them gates, since they knew what to pass inwards, and what to guard against.

Caspian had built himself a home. He wanted to live, unbound, free.

Didn't Dylan want to be free? And didn't he know what it was to be hunted?

Dylan felt a sadness then that he had often felt before at sea, but never on land. It was too large for his human mind to hold. He was sad because there were, sometimes, no good choices.

He stopped resisting the drag, and let himself be pulled in towards the light at the centre of the web of water. His skin was loud with the rushing of waves and the struggles of the creatures all around him. Much more quietly, inside, his human-self rattled at his bones.

The drag rushed him through some of the outer barriers of water, and when he passed the first of his kind it took him a moment to realise. He tensed his muscles, braking hard against the flow.

By the time he had brought himself to a halt, the wyrms were all around him, suspended above. They hung down like meat in a butcher's shop. There was a putrid feeling in the water.

He pushed his way upwards through the current. Closer, he could see that they were caught like flies, wrapped in bright ribbons of water. The ribbons gripped the wyrms in the same fierce, greedy way that the hagflesh had gripped Dylan.

He swam up to the nearest wyrm. It was not one he knew.

It was skeletally thin and pulsing strangely; it would never make it even as far as Rose's boat, against this flow.

He swam to the next. The condition was, if anything, worse. He swam to others: some already hung their heads limply, and one or two had begun to morph into something that was part-human, part-wyrm, and part meaningless decay. The sight made his heartbeat pulse loudly along his whole body. He threw all his strength against the dragging current and swam from wyrm to wyrm, searching for Mam, for Dad, both wanting to know and desperately not wanting to know.

It took a full minute of searching, and when he found Mam, he almost didn't recognise her.

She looked starved. Huge vertebrae bulged against shrivelled skin. He raised his head level with hers, and her eyes were clouded and unseeing.

In this shape, his rage was a wild thing. He shifted his weight under the rope of water that held his mam, and began looping his muscle in the rhythms and shapes he had learned, nudging and teasing the water away from her side. But he needed her to swim away when it began to loosen, and she only rolled listlessly, soon caught again by the questing tendril of water.

Dylan tried again, and again, until the tug of the current exhausted him. He kept trying long after he knew with certainty that he was too late, and that the only hope now was to poison the nál. It was his human self that kept him there. It beat against his bones insistently, intent on untying its mother – or perhaps on avoiding what came next.

In the end, it didn't matter what he decided; the force of

the water was too strong. He was pulled away like a leaf and dragged onwards, leaving Mam behind, whirling across the last short stretch to the centre of the web.

An inner ring of current guarded Caspian's nest. Dylan was deposited in this new swirl, and for a few moments he whirled around in its grip, rushing until he was no longer exactly sure where his body ended and the water began. Suddenly and ludicrously, he had a vivid memory of his human self, racing downhill on a bicycle while the light of a new morning unfolded out on all sides.

Then he was admitted into the centre, and the whirling ceased, and everything was quiet and very bright.

26

You have come.

Caspian was nowhere to be seen, in any form. Instead, Dylan was surrounded by the blinding golden light, as though he was swimming in the inside of a star. This *was* Caspian – all around him. When the voice spoke, it came from nowhere: it was already inside his mind.

This was rash. I am much too strong now. Even for you.

There was something almost sad about this. It was the sadness of somebody with no good choices. Dylan couldn't speak, and found he couldn't move either; he was held still, as though he had been pinned in place for examination in the light.

It was a long time before the voice spoke again. As though Dylan's eyes were adjusting to the light, he began to see the nál's other forms as the water circled him. Often, he was surrounded by the coils of a great serpent. But sometimes there were hoofs, tentacles, fins, teeth. All of it was blinding light, constantly shifting shape, seething restlessly.

You are not as strong as the last one, it said at last. *The one that bound me first.*

For a moment, the light shimmered, and some of it condensed in front of Dylan into a familiar shape. It was Caspian, if Caspian had been the size of a seamount and the colour of the sun.

Parts of me are sorry, Dylan Pade. But they are the weaker parts of me. And I am strong again now. Without your kind, there will be nothing that threatens me.

Dylan could not speak, in his wyrm form, but perhaps this great serpent knew his mind. *Your spirit would have given the hag enormous power*, it said. *It would still have been a danger to me. Had your sister stayed at the wreck her doubled spirit would have fused with the spirit of the dead there, with what you call wreck-water, and that would have made an even greater terror. It is your spirits I fear, and spirit cannot be destroyed. I must be the one to consume you.* And Caspian reached out a hand, which became a tendril of golden water . . .

. . . and the water was wrapping itself around Dylan, looping around his long body, so silken and cool it could almost have been soothing, if Dylan's huge heartbeats were not a warning signal thrumming through every coil of his flesh . . .

For the first moments, Dylan struggled. He was surprised to find that he was strong enough to make things meaningfully harder for the nál; he could feel that the dragging current was exhausting its power, and understood for the first time how much it weakened itself, peeling off so many pieces of itself to pull and trap and fight. It wanted to stop. It wanted to live without fear, whole.

But even if he could tire it, he couldn't defeat it. And it was drawing in Tor-Meriel and Uncle Firth and Rose and innocent landmen – and other pieces were holding Mam and Dad, and all his helpless kind – and all he had to do, to end it all, was give in.

He let himself fall limp.

The tendrils of water tightened, and the nál began to feed.

Dylan's human spirit left him slowly, in a giddy dream that spiralled inwards.

It began on a small boat that drifted over a sea like buttery candlelight. And there was the other pool of light too, the lamplight of his last long vigil at the cottage, fretting for his family. The two flickered in and out of one another: the start and the finish of the end, the long golden evening of his human life.

Then the gold faded to grey, the grey SS *Rose Marie* on the great grey sea, and he was watched from the deck by his uncle's silver eyes, which were Mam's eyes, and the eyes of everyone who loved him. Who *had* loved him. He seemed to watch the ship getting smaller, sailing to a horizon where he could no longer follow.

The grey sea turned red, and frothed and churned, and he was lost in a whirlpool of it, and he could not shake that part of the dream for an immeasurably long time. Figures tried to reach him, Mam Dad Meriel Tor Firth Grandpa, but they could never swim close enough.

When he was released again he was small, on Grandpa Willig's boat. He was on the deck coming back from the water, and the creaky plank creaked, and the lamp over the door shone warmly against a purple evening. His skin and mind felt clean and new. He opened the door to the smell of Uncle Firth's trout stew, and the adults were in huddled discussion, which stopped as soon as he came in, and they all looked up at him guiltily . . .

. . . he was in bed crying, and Tor was shouting downstairs, shouting that he had bitten Meriel and he didn't know what he was doing and he shouldn't be allowed to come to sea with them, he wasn't safe . . .

. . . he was a toddler, and he was watching landmen in the loch, and he was asking Dad why they didn't change shape. And Dad said they were different. And Dylan was sorry for them, and so happy that he was normal, and not different like them . . .

. . . he was a baby, clutched to a woman's chest. His whole body ached from the inside out, and he cried and cried and cried.

'He won't stop, Doug,' sobbed the woman. 'He's hurting so much. My poor baby. What can we do?' And a man's arms took him, and rocked him, but the ache wouldn't stop, not ever . . .

. . . and Dylan Pade's silver-laced human spirit left him and entered entirely into the nál Caspian; and the nál howled in agony, and all the sea shook with the sound.

The wyrm found himself released on to the seabed. There was a sudden deafness, as though a part of him that had always been listening to an elsewhere was gone. He no longer knew if it was day or night; he had always known what the sun above was doing, as clearly as he knew the turning of the tide.

He reached for his own small name, and found it missing.

Above him, a golden light was fading, like the end of a long bright day. Sea creatures drifted down to the bed, dazed. He felt a web of countless currents falling slack.

He watched the nearest threads of current. They seemed to be solidifying as they drifted to the seabed: forming thin tendrils, almost-transparent, small and snake-like and harmless. New eels, he realised. Beginning their lives in the Sargasso Sea. His heart was suddenly full: he wanted, so badly, to tell . . . someone. Who was it?

He could not move. Overhead, a pack of long black shapes snaked upwards to the water's surface, thin and ragged and determined. They were large and graceful. Water-dragons, knuckers, uilebheists, loch monsters, wyrms: the Weards of the Sea, half remembered by the world above.

The wyrm on the seabed wanted to call out, but wyrms have no voices. He wanted to swim up to them, but his body was limp and broken. With an effort, he lifted a great head, barely swirling the sand around him.

It was impossible to tell which of the shadows above were his own kin as they all swam away, heading for the surface, and the world above.

27

The fading of the golden light was long and stuttering. At last there was only a small coil of gold left in the mud, like a weed: not quite dead, but reduced to a seed of itself. The Sea returned, without fanfare, to its old paths.

The plains at the bottom of the world were black again. The grains of sand shifted sometimes under the wyrm's belly, as bottom-dwellers scuttled or slid through the silt beneath. Its skin told it when unseen creatures moved past in the bone-cold water, and every now and then one would wink with blue-green lights; occasional shudders announced that one had fought another, and something had died. There are not many good choices on the deep plains.

The wyrm couldn't tell if it spent hours or days there, feeling its strength return. It would have known once, when it could feel the passage of day and night, in its other form. It would have known then, too, the name for the sadness it felt, and the cause. It was sure it had suffered a great loss. But the more the black hours drifted past, the less it could remember.

In the end, it only knew that it was hungry, and would prefer to be lying in some sort of cavern where the sea did not roll against its side so incessantly. It picked itself up from the mud, and climbed for higher water, to hunt for a means of living.

Everything wants to live. The wyrm had a feeling, like an echo in its bones, that it used to want more than that. But what, exactly, it could not now recall.

14 Gooley Street
London
2nd November 1929

Dear Dylan,

Your uncle gave me this address to write to. He thinks you might just be injured, and your family might find you, and he says I should write in case. I am not sure whether he believes that, or is just being kind.

This is my sixth attempt at a beginning. I'm sure I am not the first girl to have trouble knowing what to say in a letter like this. But I think it is <u>quite</u> unusual to be unsure whether the recipient is alive and injured somewhere, or permanently changed into a water-dragon, or dead. When I think you might be gone, I start writing the most awfully soppy things. And then I remember that you might actually read this after all, and I have to cross it all out and start again.

I know you said not to wait for you on the lifeboat, but I did. The sea turned grey and still, and everything was awfully quiet, and I was desperate for proof that you were all right. But the others in the boat were terribly unwell, and in the end I knew I had to get them to the ship. A few were well enough to help me row. Most were barely conscious. It was awful, heaving across the ocean with a boat full of naked moaning people, all squirming and rolling their eyes and looking like they might die at any moment. I began to think the whole thing might be a nightmare, and at any moment I'd wake up.

Now all your kind have gone again, and it feels even more like a dream. Your parents went back to sea to find you, as soon as they were conscious and understood what had happened. The others stayed on the ship until we docked in New York, but they've gone now to recover on the lakes here. The men of the Rose Marie have come up with a hundred stories to account for the strange refugees, and the strange sea. None of them are even close to the truth. It would be funny if it wasn't so awful to listen to them and feel so completely alone.

I'm in the infirmary. They have put me here because I am claiming I have lost my memory, and generally acting like a dolt. I didn't know what else to say when Father was quizzing me on why I was in the boat with you, and what happened while we were there ... It was a jolly stupid lie but I can't think of anything better, and he can't think of anything to do except stick me in here and have the doctor fuss around me. So now I have to look at the beds where you and your sister were, empty and tidily made, like you were never here.

I have been trying to imagine how I must have seemed to you. We knew each other so little. For me, you seemed like someone I had always known was going to arrive. I spent half my life thinking about the secrets I was sure were in the sea, and the other half dreaming that someone fascinating would come on board one day and sweep me away somehow to a different life. Every time we set sail, yet again, without anybody interesting on board, I would feel terribly dreary. And then this time – there you were.

I was awfully brazen, I think. I just felt so <u>certain</u>. Even when you were furious with me and I didn't know why, I just felt absolutely certain I could unravel it all and make things *all right. And then when you needed someone to go into the boat with you, I was just certain I could do that too, and that everything would work out for the best. But then you kissed me and – this is going to sound silly – I suddenly truly understood that you are a real person, not just a character in the story of my life, and that anything could happen. That was the first time I was afraid.*

I am really afraid now. I feel this dreadful certainty that you are gone, and I won't see you again, and I won't ever know exactly what happened to you . . . If you are alive, please write to me at the address above. I can check for post there whenever we dock in London. I will be looking out for your letter.

I don't know what else to say.

Your friend (who is definitely <u>not</u> a hag),
Rose Marie x

4th December 1929

Kelda,

Thank you for letting me know you're all back home and safe from the nál binding. I know it is barely alive now, but I still don't like the thought of you all anywhere near that thing. I still see its merfolk-shape in my dreams, smiling at me. Let us hope it's now safely bound for a long time yet.

I hope this letter reaches you before you return to sea. I am only your foolish little brother, but I feel duty-bound to give you some advice: you and Douglas cannot sustain the search at this intensity. I am worried for you, and your weakening land selves. You know that it's dangerous to spend so much time in your other form, but I don't think you see how much you are already sickening. Spend more time on land – if not for yourself, then for Morgen (did she choose the new name herself? A wonderful, strong sea name). She is handling the newly doubled sea-spirit bravely, and I know she doesn't want to worry you, but she needs guidance. If Dylan is out there to be found, he will still be there tomorrow, and he would want you to take care.

I know you will be cross about this advice, which is why I have written this in a letter like a big coward, because I am indeed your foolish little brother. I look forward to my telling-off.

I will be with you again in three weeks. I'll be stopping my boat at the Kentons', the Plovers' and Isla's, so please send any news to all three.

Thinking of you, and him, more than I can say. Look after yourself, Kelda, please. We all love you and need you.

River keep you,
Firth

28

The wyrm was half sleeping in the kelp forests of the Bering Sea. It only ever half slept: nothing would attack its flesh, but it only had one spirit now, and had to be wary. It kept to the good water around the coastal shelves and seamounts and ridges — here was a favourite spot, where volcanos grew up on all sides, appearing above the sea as islands — and it preferred the colder waters, which deterred many of the weaker spirit-eaters.

It had lain here half sleeping for some time; brittle stars had begun to settle on its sides and back, and the mud beneath had moulded to its great shape. Between the high stalks of kelp, light came and went in folds.

One half-open eye caught the movement of a shadow, and it seemed faster and sharper than the swaying shadows of the kelp. The wyrm opened its eyes, and listened to its skin.

There was something in the kelp.

Before the wyrm could move, the something darted out: a shadow that was half-boy, half-fish, and carrying a knife. It drew this against the wyrm's side, then pushed against the great body as though trying to close the wound it had just made.

The wyrm shook itself from the seabed, and snarled its double jaws. Insanely, the figure hung on. It seemed to be trying to crush itself into the wound. The wyrm turned its head, but the figure was a little too close for its jaws to reach; so it launched its long body from the seabed, and shook violently.

The figure held on grimly, and at the wound, something was coursing through the wyrm like electricity. Then at last the figure gave in, and swam away with the speed of a fierce ocean current.

The wyrm gave chase. Its attacker skimmed up the rocky slopes of a volcano, towards the surface water. The wyrm pointed its body into a vertical line, and followed.

The figure broke through the waves. The wyrm had not surfaced for a long time, and for a moment, the bright light made it hesitate. But something else inside it seemed to be stirring, and reaching for the light, so it pushed onwards, and broke through the foam . . .

. . . and Dylan was on an unknown coast. It was like waking, his thoughts arriving piece by piece: there, those were his small toes on the round grey stones. There, that was land-light, steady and still in the way that sea-light never was. He was Dylan.

Caspian lay some way away from him on the stones, dagger drawn. Folds of grey mountainside rose behind him. There was no one else around them besides the colonies of seabirds overhead, who called to each other, unconcerned by the new arrivals on the shore below.

Dylan rolled away, scrambling for a weapon. Should he still be wearing his bandoleer? He didn't remember where he had lost it. He didn't know where he was.

'My knife is only for self-defence,' said Caspian. 'I do not want to hurt you.'

Dylan didn't know much, just then, but he knew that this was preposterous. 'You killed me.'

'I took your human self,' Caspian corrected.

'I *am* my . . .' Dylan trailed off, as he remembered that he was human again right now, which undermined the point he wanted to make – and raised questions.

'I have given it back,' said Caspian. His face was serious, but his eyes looked suspiciously like he was laughing – or at least, glad – as Dylan felt the edges of his own arms incredulously. Dylan saw the gladness, and tensed warily; he gathered himself to a squat on the ground, ready to dive back into the ocean. The laughter left Caspian's eyes.

'I gave it back by blood,' he said. He raised an arm, showing Dylan the knife-wound he had made. 'I am not sure what your kind know of these things . . . I had subsumed your spirit into mine, and if two bloods contain like spirit, there can be a transference . . .'

Affinity of spirit, Tor-Meriel had called it. Dylan nodded warily, but did not drop from his ready squat.

'I have searched for you a long time,' said Caspian. 'It is much harder to feel where you are in the water, without both your selves. I was surprised how hard it was.' When Dylan didn't reply, he went on: 'Your family live. Almost all the wyrms do. I met them again; they returned to bind me. For those that died, I am sorry.'

'How are you here?'

'Already my binding loosens. No, do not be alarmed!' he added, seeing Dylan's face. 'It is not loose enough for me to grow strong. It will keep me weak for some time. But it is enough for my smaller forms to live freely.' He gestured to his chest with the hand that didn't hold the dagger. 'This is who I most often am, between the outbursts of my other self, and the times when I am newly bound by your kind and become nothing for a while.'

There was a long silence. Dylan knew he should leave for the sea, where – if Caspian was telling the truth – he was easily the stronger of the two of them. But he hadn't felt sunlight or quiet skin in a long time, and he didn't want to go back. Not yet.

'The stronger part of me hates your kind,' said Caspian mildly. 'You are a threat to its existence.'

'You talk like it wasn't you . . .'

'I do not mean to. I accept that it is part of me. When it is ascendent, it is hard for me to act against its desires.'

Dylan understood this, and didn't want to. He was silent.

'The weaker part of me understands balance,' Caspian went on. 'It wills what is good for the sea, and it knows that my freedom is too costly – at least, for now.'

'For now?' said Dylan.

Caspian's eyes certainly smiled then. 'Ah, I have alarmed you again,' he said. 'I forget how young you are. I do not expect this to change in many lifetimes. But I have known other seas, and times without fish or men, and I expect to know them again.'

Dylan stared. Somehow, despite everything, he was unable to stop seeing Caspian as a teenage merfolk boy. 'How old are you?' he said.

'I told you once that I do not know,' said Caspian, 'and that was true.' He looked up at the sky a few moments, as though the passage of the sun might answer the question. 'I think,' he said, 'I may be as old as the sea. I wonder sometimes if I am a part of it.'

'You don't know?'

'Do you know what *you* are?'

Dylan was silent at that, because he was feeling his small skin like a new miracle, and he knew that he didn't have a good answer. For a few moments they both stayed poised in wary defence, watching each other. Dylan found he was struggling to feel hostile to Caspian – to *this* Caspian. He hated the blinding golden light in the Sargasso Sea, fiercely, but he could not put the two together in his head. And after all, didn't he know what it was to have a monstrous side?

'Where do you live, in this form?' he asked.

Caspian shook his head. 'Dylan, we speak in peace now, but I am not a fool.'

'No – but I mean – when you're human, do you have a different home . . . ?' He was envisaging lonely kelp forests and dark caves, and it seemed unbearably sad – but the sadness, he realised, was coming from his own memories. How long had he been at sea?

Caspian was shaking his head again. 'I am never human.'

'Merfolk are human.'

'But I am not merfolk. This is only a shape. My mind is not like yours, even when I am weak.'

Dylan's own mind was racing now, urged on by the exhilaration of new blood moving around a new body. 'But if we could find a way to kill your other self for good, you wouldn't have to be in exile . . . ?'

Caspian bared his teeth then, in an entirely inhuman way, and Dylan recoiled, falling backwards from his squat. They stared at each other, and there was a moment's quiet before Caspian replied.

'I would not destroy a part of myself,' he said, 'for anything at all.'

'But if it meant you could have a home . . . ?'

'I have a home. It is the sea.'

'That seems so sad.'

'You are so much more human than you realise,' said Caspian. 'It is not sad to me.'

Overhead, bird called to bird, and one flapped across the sky to meet the other. Dylan tried to sort out the muddle of new thoughts fluttering inside him. It was so long since his thoughts had been this small and busy – human thoughts swarmed like a shoal of fish, and it was overwhelming.

'Do not attempt to destroy yourself again,' said Caspian. 'You are part of the balance. And you will be Weard now that your sisters are one.'

Dylan considered this. He found he was less afraid of himself than he had been before. 'I can remember it all much more clearly now,' he said. 'I remember what I was doing, and thinking . . .'

'You did not have these memories before?'

'It was always blurry.'

Caspian considered this. 'I was surprised how weak your sea-self was, when I consumed you. You have spent too little time at sea, I think, for such a large spirit. Does it hurt you, on land?'

Dylan nodded.

'I understand this,' said Caspian. 'My other self hurts, when it is bound. Let your sea-self have its freedom, and it will not hurt you. It will grow properly, and be a part of you. Otherwise, it will always be out of your control.'

Dylan nodded again. 'It feels different already, after being at sea so long,' he said. 'I've never done that – I've always been afraid of it. It was so strong. I only went to sea when I had to.'

Caspian inclined his head. 'Understandable,' he said, with the smiling eyes.

It was the smiling eyes that made it impossible for Dylan to abandon Caspian – this human-seeming Caspian – this boy. He leaned forward earnestly. 'Couldn't you live near the coasts when you're in this shape?' he said. 'Then you could warn us when you're getting strong again, but until then, maybe the folk . . .'

'Not every Weard would treat me so generously, I think. In this form, I am easily destroyed.'

'But you could trust some of us. You shouldn't have to exile yourself entirely.'

'What interesting advice you give,' said Caspian slyly. 'If I was a shapeshifter with a truly human side, I would certainly listen to it.' He pushed himself up, and looked out to sea, as though something was calling him; then he sheathed his dagger in his bandoleer. 'You do not understand me,' he said, without regret. 'We are too different. But I am glad to have known you, Dylan Pade. Humans are a very beautiful and strange part of the present balance.'

Just like that, Caspian was pushing his palms against the stones, and swinging himself towards the sea. Dylan felt a sudden panic, a backwards homesickness, at the idea of being left alone here on this cold and stony shore.

'Wait!' he said. 'Will I see you again?'

'I imagine you will come to bind me.'

'But like this, I mean.'

Caspian shrugged. 'I am not a future-teller.' He clasped one fist to his chest, and bowed his head. 'Dylan Pade,' he said, 'Child of the Weard.'

Dylan clutched an answering fist to his own chest, and for a moment he couldn't speak, voiceless as a wyrm again. The silver of Caspian's tail and the pale white of his skin slipped quietly into the white-grey waves. They swallowed him without pausing in their rhythm.

'Caspian,' Dylan replied, 'nál of the Sargasso Sea.'

29

When he was almost home, Dylan pulled himself from the water to a blush pink shore, overlooked by red cliffs, where the cave mouths waited. He scrambled up the marram grass to the most promisingly forbidden of the caves, and looked in. The throaty tunnel gaped at him, and closed into darkness.

He wasn't sure why he had wanted to see it. His human-self had strange urges too, sometimes. He took one last long look at the retreating dark; he thought of shouting out to hear the echoes, like they had when they were children, but he didn't like to disturb that nightmare place. Instead, he trod away softly, back on to the sand, and out into the sea.

It was the most familiar journey in his world: out of the sea into River Ness, through to Loch Dochfour, on into Loch Ness. The salt water lightened to fresh river water, then grew heavy again with peat, as the waters of Loch Ness folded about him like velvet.

He transformed on his own shore, and made his way under whispering pines, to the gingerbread cottage. On his way here, his happiness had at times been dizzying. Now that he had arrived, he still felt glad, but it was a quiet gladness – like the spreading warmth of a summer evening. It felt, now, as though there had never been any possibility he would *not* come back to this place. It was the peculiar happiness of a home, which is sometimes a sadness too: the way it gives solidity to small lives, and makes their fleeting details feel like laws of nature.

Smiling, Dylan opened the door.

Sunlight went in ahead of him, breaking open the gloom that filtered through the window's shutters. The old table stood, and the armchairs. But besides this, the room was empty. The smell of pine tar was faint, overlayed with a much heavier smell of dust.

'Hello?' he called.

He walked out of the empty front room, and looked in at the empty kitchen. The empty utility room had suffered a blow to its skylight from a tree branch, and the scent of outside poured in. Absurdly, Dylan checked the toilet and the forge. He went upstairs to look in bedrooms, empty besides the beds.

In Mam and Dad's room he stood looking at the bed he had curled up on, when he was smaller, for stories. It had clearly not been used for some time.

He took a deep breath. They had probably just gone somewhere, and he could find out where; he could write to Auntie Isla's house, or one of the others on their emergency list of addresses. But still, he found himself looking at his hands, searching for signs of aging. He was certainly still young – surely his human body would age, even if he was at sea? Surely he hadn't been away their whole lifetimes?

For completeness, he climbed the last flight of stairs, to his own room. Here, his breath caught. Nothing here had changed. His blankets were on the bed, and his books and lamp were on the chest of drawers. The window shutters were open, looking out over the loch.

On the bed was the case he had taken to London, and onwards to the SS *Rose Marie*. On top of the case there were two envelopes.

He picked up the one on top. In Mam's handwriting, it said: *For Dylan*. He tore it open.

> *Dylan, my love,*
>
> *It's too hard for us to stay here. It's so full of our memories of you. We are moving to a new place on Loch Morar, and we are going to try and be happy there. But I will never stop thinking of you, and if you should ever come home to us, please come and find us there. I have drawn a map below. I will be waiting – every day – always.*
>
> *Your loving,*
> *Mam*

Dylan read it several times, until tears blurred the words. He blinked them away, and looked at the second letter: the postmark announced it as an arrival from the United States of America. He tore it open, read it, and smiled.

He sat on his bed, and memorised the map. Then he stood, and placed both letters very carefully back on the case. He would reply to the second soon; thinking about it gave him a buzzy, glowing feeling. He took a fly-silk bag and an old bandoleer from his drawers, and he put some clothes in the bag. He would have to come back for the rest of his things later, with the boat.

But first, he had to finish his journey home.

The cottage, which just a moment ago had seemed like the inevitable end of all his adventures, now already seemed hollowed out. He went down the familiar creaks and thuds of the stairs, past Mam and Dad's room and Meriel and Tor's room, down into the front room below. He crossed over to the door, then hesitated.

'Thank you,' he said.

The cottage didn't reply. It was, after all, only a house.

Amid the usual wind rustling in the pines, Dylan thought he heard something, and it brought him to a sharp stop. Some of that wind had been, quite distinctly, annoying.

He turned and smiled at the morose man who stood behind him, spreading its hands.

'Hello,' he said. 'I wondered if I'd see you again.'

'Dylan Pade,' said the man.

'Yep,' said Dylan. 'That's me.'

The man nodded once, as though this had been the confirmation he needed. Then there was a gust of wind – which smelled like the sharp edge of spring when it has just begun, and is powerful and strange and not entirely kind – not entirely human. The man was gone.

'Thank you,' said Dylan.

The kelpie didn't reply, even more emphatically than the cottage. Dylan smiled to himself, and left for the water.

30

The waters of Loch Morar were clearer and lighter than Loch Ness, and ran across Dylan's skin as gently as silk. He came ashore on grass, and looked back: the day was bright now, and the loch held all the sky between its banks. It was, he thought, a good choice.

He took his clothes from the bag on his bandoleer, dressed, and set out for home.

On the north-eastern shore, where Mam had marked the spot, a little grey stone house stood. And between Dylan and the house, Tor-Meriel knelt on the grass, sorting through a collecting-basket full of herbs.

Dylan wondered whether to shout out. But he didn't know what to say – 'Hello!' seemed ludicrous. So he kept walking closer, and waited for her to notice, savouring the moment. Her plaits were swinging in their earnest way, and she was doing the half-whispering, half-breathing thing that both twins did when they were concentrating.

He was only a few steps away when she looked up. She sprang to her feet, and for a few seconds she only stared; then she threw her arms around him, with all of Meriel's fierceness and all of Tor's abandon.

'Dylanitssreallyyouohriver, oh, Dylan,' she said, mostly into his shoulder. Dylan said something equally incoherent back. It didn't matter particularly, because he had known his sisters longer than words.

At last she pulled away, but kept hold of his hand, tugging. 'Come on,' she said, 'you have to come and see everyone. Oh, their faces! Uncle Firth's here too. I think he'll probably faint . . .'

And she pushed open the front door, still holding on to Dylan with her other hand. This new house smelled like their old one – pine tar and soap. Mam had her back to them, writing something in a journal. Over the top of an armchair, Dylan saw the hedgehog-head of Uncle Firth.

Mam turned first, and for a moment before she saw him, Dylan saw the face she wore now when she was doing nothing in particular. It was as though the painful softness in her eyes had spread: her expression was nothing but softness now, the hard determination all gone.

Then she saw him, and she shrieked so loudly that Uncle Firth stood at once, saying, 'What – ?' – and a door behind her opened hurriedly, and Dad said, 'Kelda, are you – ?'

And then everybody was saying his name at once, and coming forward to hold on to him, and never let him go.

'Hi,' said Dylan, from somewhere among them all. 'I'm home.'

Deep in his bones, something inside him roared.

Acknowledgements

Sometimes the book you are writing is so tightly woven into the life you are living that it's hard to know where to stop the thank yous. So I will just *start* them, and see what happens.

Thank you to Bryony Woods, my agent, for being the engine behind this and so many other incredible opportunities. Thank you to my editors, Chloe Sackur and Charlie Sheppard, for their invaluable input as this book metamorphosed (as all good sea creatures must); and thank you to Eloise Wilson for the meticulous copy edit.

Thank you Kate Grove for the design, Thy Bui for the cover, and Rebecca Freeman for the map. I will treasure this beautiful book you all made.

Thanks and grateful hugs to readers who gave feedback along the way: Caitlin Campbell, Anya Glazer, Polly Meyrick, Sam Plumb, Erin Simmons, Dylan Townley, Maddy Vierbuchen and Alice Winn.

And thank you Maddy, Polly and Luke for living with me while I wrote this. No household could be more bountiful in kindness and teabags, and it has meant the world. (I would thank Zaki too, but it would only make him furious.)

ON SILVER TIDES

SYLVIA BISHOP

'The timeless power and craftsmanship of a classic'
SUNDAY TIMES, BOOK OF THE WEEK

'Will fill you with wonder' ANN SEI LIN

Kelda and her family are silvermen, a hidden people who have the ability to swim like fish and breathe through their skin. Yet Kelda's little sister is born different. The family must protect her from the suspicions of their community – for her very existence is forbidden and the whole family is in danger. When betrayal comes, the girls escape on a desperate journey across Britain's waterways. To save her sister, Kelda must brave monstrous creatures at every turn, and delve into the darkest depths of her kind's secret history . . .

NOMINATED FOR THE CARNEGIE MEDAL FOR WRITING

WORLD WEAVERS

SAM GAYTON

Hush and Matilda have been hiding out in a pocket world, ever since the war started. Ever since Dustbowl fell. Ever since what happened to Ma. But when a boy with no memory crosses into their reality, the sisters must confront their past, each other, and the intoxicating power that has torn their lives apart ... the power known as worldweaving.

'Wildly original adventure from an author whose imagination seems boundless' *Lovereading*

9781839131264

Yours from the Tower

SALLY NICHOLLS

1896. Tirzah, Sophia and Polly are best friends who've left boarding school and gone back to very different lives. Polly is teaching in an orphanage. Sophia is looking for a rich husband at the London Season. And Tirzah is stuck acting as an unpaid companion to her grandmother. In a series of letters, they share their hopes, their frustrations, their dramas ... and their romances. Can these three very different young women find happiness?

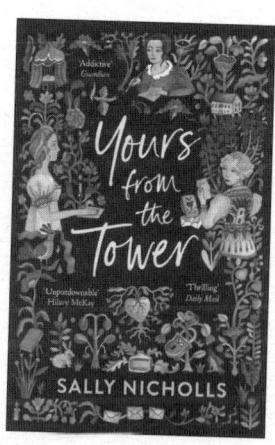

'An addictive, romantic epistolary novel' *Guardian*

'I loved this book. An unputdownable friendship story' Hilary McKay